Workshop on Language in Social Media 2011

(LSM 2011)

Held at ACL HLT 2011

Portland, Oregon, USA
23 June 2011

ISBN: 978-1-61839-241-1

Printed from e-media with permission by:

Curran Associates, Inc.
57 Morehouse Lane
Red Hook, NY 12571

CURRAN ASSOCIATES INC. proceedings.com

Some format issues inherent in the e-media version may also appear in this print version.

Printed by Curran Associates, Inc. (2011)

Association for Computational Linguistics
209 N. Eighth Street
Stroudsburg, Pennsylvania 18360

Phone: 1-570-476-8006
Fax: 1-570-476-0860

acl@aclweb.org

Additional copies of this publication are available from:

Curran Associates, Inc.
57 Morehouse Lane
Red Hook, NY 12571 USA
Phone: 845-758-0400
Fax: 845-758-2634
Email: curran@proceedings.com
Web: www.proceedings.com

Introduction

Welcome to the ACL Workshop on Language in Social Media (LSM 2011)!

Over the last few years, there has been a growing public and enterprise interest in 'social media' and their role in modern society. At the heart of this interest is the ability for users to create and share content via a variety of platforms such as blogs, micro-blogs, collaborative wikis, multimedia sharing sites, social networking sites etc. The volume and variety of user-generated content (UGC) and the user participation network behind it are creating new opportunities for understanding web-based practices and building socially intelligent and personalized applications. Investigations around social data can be broadly categorized along the following dimensions:
(a) understanding aspects of the user-generated content
(b) modeling and observing the user network that the content is generated in and
(c) characterizing individuals and groups that produce and consume the content.

The goals for this workshop are to focus on sharing research efforts and results in the area of understanding language usage on social media.

While there is a rich body of previous work in processing textual content, certain characteristics of UGC on social media introduce challenges in their analyses. A large portion of language found in UGC is in the Informal English domain — a blend of abbreviations, slang and context specific terms; lacking in sufficient context and regularities and delivered with an indifferent approach to grammar and spelling. Traditional content analysis techniques developed for a more formal genre like news, Wikipedia or scientific articles do not necessarily translate well to UGC. Consequently, well-understood problems such as information extraction, search or monetization on the Web are facing pertinent challenges and need to be revisited.

Meena Nagarajan and Michael Gamon

Organizers:

Meena Nagarajan (IBM Research)
Michael Gamon (Microsoft Research)

Program Committee:

John Breslin (University of Galway)
Cindy Chung (University of Texas)
Munmun De Choudhury (Arizona State University)
Cristian Danescu-Niculescu-Mizil (Cornell University)
Susan Dumais (Microsoft Research)
Jennifer Foster (Dublin City University)
Sam Gosling (University of Texas)
Julia Grace (IBM Research)
Daniel Gruhl (IBM Research)
Kevin Haas (Microsoft)
Emre Kiciman (Microsoft Research)
Nicolas Nicolov (Microsoft)
Daniel Ramage (Stanford University)
Alan Ritter (University of Washington)
Christine Robson (IBM Research)
Hassan Sayyadi (University of Maryland)
Valerie Shalin (Wright State University)
Amit Sheth (Wright State University)
Ian Soboroff (NIST)
Hari Sundaram (Arizona State University)
Scott Spangler (IBM Research)
Smaranda Muresan (Rutgers University)

Additional Reviewers:

Kristina Toutanova (Microsoft Research)
Josephine Griffith (NUI Galway)
Hemant Purohit (Wright State University)
Lu Chen (Wright State University)
Ashutosh Jadhav (Wright State University)

Invited Speaker:

Susan C. Herring (Indiana University)

Table of Contents

Conference Program

9:00	**Opening remarks**

Keynote

9:15 *Automating Analysis of Social Media Communication: Insights from CMDA*
Susan Herring

10:15 **Coffee break**

Session 1

10:30 *How can you say such things?!?: Recognizing Disagreement in Informal Political Argument*
Rob Abbott, Marilyn Walker, Pranav Anand, Jean E. Fox Tree, Robeson Bowmani and Joseph King

11:00 *What pushes their buttons? Predicting comment polarity from the content of political blog posts*
Ramnath Balasubramanyan, William W. Cohen, Doug Pierce and David P. Redlawsk

11:30 *Contextual Bearing on Linguistic Variation in Social Media*
Stephan Gouws, Donald Metzler, Congxing Cai and Eduard Hovy

12:00 *Sentiment Analysis of Twitter Data*
Apoorv Agarwal, Boyi Xie, Ilia Vovsha, Owen Rambow and Rebecca Passonneau

12:30 **Lunch break**

Session 2

1:30 *Detecting Forum Authority Claims in Online Discussions*
Alex Marin, Bin Zhang and Mari Ostendorf

2:00 *Annotating Social Acts: Authority Claims and Alignment Moves in Wikipedia Talk Pages*
Emily M. Bender, Jonathan T. Morgan, Meghan Oxley, Mark Zachry, Brian Hutchinson, Alex Marin, Bin Zhang and Mari Ostendorf

2:30 *Analyzing the Dynamic Evolution of Hashtags on Twitter: a Language-Based Approach*
Evandro Cunha, Gabriel Magno, Giovanni Comarela, Virgilio Almeida, Marcos André Gonçalves and Fabricio Benevenuto

3:00 *Why is "SXSW" trending? Exploring Multiple Text Sources for Twitter Topic Summarization*
Fei Liu, Yang Liu and Fuliang Weng

Session 3

4:00 *Language use as a reflection of socialization in online communities*
Dong Nguyen and Carolyn P. Rosé

4:30 *Email Formality in the Workplace: A Case Study on the Enron Corpus*
Kelly Peterson, Matt Hohensee and Fei Xia

5:00 **Discussion and Closing Remarks**

Keynote

Automating Analysis of Social Media Communication: Insights from CMDA

Susan C. Herring
School of Library & Information Science and Department of Linguistics
Indiana University
Bloomington
herring@indiana.edu

Abstract

A growing body of research analyzes the linguistic and discourse properties of communication in online social media. Most of the analysis, especially at the discourse level, is done manually by human researchers. This talk explores how the findings and techniques of computer-mediated discourse analysis (CMDA), a paradigm I have been developing and teaching for 18 years, can inform computational approaches to communication in social media. I start by reviewing established automation approaches, which mainly focus on structural linguistic phenomena, and emergent approaches, such as machine learning models that identify semantically- and pragmatically-richer phenomena, through the lens of CMDA, pointing out the strengths and limitations of each. The basic problem is that patterns in the discourse of social media users can be identified by humans that do not appear to lend themselves to reliable automated identification using existing approaches. To begin to address this problem, I draw on examples of recent work on Twitter, Wikipedia, and web-based discussion forums to suggest an approach that synthesizes linguistically-informed manual analysis and existing automated techniques. I consider how such an approach could scale up, while still making use of human analysts, and I identify a number of real-world problems that automated CMDA could help address.

How can you say such things?!?: Recognizing Disagreement in Informal Political Argument

Rob Abbott, Marilyn Walker, Pranav Anand, Jean E. Fox Tree, Robeson Bowmani, and Joseph King
University of California Santa Cruz
abbott|maw@soe.ucsc.edu, panand|foxtree@ucsc.edu

Abstract

The recent proliferation of political and social forums has given rise to a wealth of freely accessible naturalistic arguments. People can "talk" to anyone they want, at any time, in any location, about any topic. Here we use a Mechanical Turk annotated corpus of forum discussions as a gold standard for the recognition of disagreement in online ideological forums. We analyze the utility of meta-post features, contextual features, dependency features and word-based features for signaling the disagreement relation. We show that using contextual and dialogic features we can achieve accuracies up to 68% as compared to a unigram baseline of 63%.

1 Introduction

The recent proliferation of political and social forums has given rise to a wealth of freely accessible naturalistic arguments. People can "talk" to anyone they want, at any time, in any location, about any topic. Their conversations range from current political topics such as national health care to religious questions such as the meaning of biblical passages. See Figure 1. We aim to automatically derive representations of the discourse structure of such arguments and to gain a deeper theoretical and empirical understanding of the linguistic reflexes of perlocutionary acts such as persuasion (Austin, 1965).

The study of the structure of argumentative communication has a long lineage in psychology (Cialdini, 2000) and rhetoric (Hunter, 1987), but the historical lack of a large corpus of naturalistic examples has limited empirical work to a handful of genres (e.g., editorials or simulated negotiations). Argumentation is above all tactical. Thus being able to effectively model it would afford us a glimpse of pragmatics beyond the conversational turn. More practically, an increasing portion of information and opinion exchange online occurs in natural dialogue, in forums, in webpage comments, and in the back

Topic	Q-R: Post
Evolution	**Q:** How can you say such things? The Bible says that God CREATED over and OVER and OVER again! And you reject that and say that everything came about by evolution? If you reject the literal account of the Creation in Genesis, you are saying that God is a liar! If you cannot trust God's Word from the first verse, how can you know that the rest of it can be trusted? **R:** It's not a literal account unless you interpret it that way.
Gay marriage	**Q:** Gavin Newsom- I expected more from him when I supported him in the 2003 election. He showed himself as a family-man/Catholic, but he ended up being the exact oppisate, supporting abortion, and giving homosexuals marriage licenses. I love San Francisco, but I hate the people. Sometimes, the people make me want to move to Sacramento or DC to fix things up. **R:** And what is wrong with giving homosexuals the right to settle down with the person they love? What is it to you if a few limp-wrists get married in San Francisco? Homosexuals are people, too, who take out their garbage, pay their taxes, go to work, take care of their dogs, and what they do in their bedroom is none of your business.
Abortion	**Q:** Equality is not defined by you or me. It is defined by the Creator who created men. **R:** Actually I think it is defined by the creator who created all women. But in reality your opinion is gibberish. Equality is, like every other word, defined by the people who use the language. Currently it means "the same". People aren't equal because they are not all the same. Any attempt to argue otherwise is a display of gross stupidity.

Figure 1: Sample Quote/Response Pairs

and forth of short messages (e.g., Facebook status updates, tweets, etc.) Effective models of argumentative discourse thus have clear applications in automatic summarization, information retrieval, or predicting real-world events such as how well a new product is being received or the outcome of a popular vote on a topic (Bollen et al., 2011).

In this paper, we focus on an important initial task for the recognition of argumentative structure: automatic identification of agreement and disagreement. We introduce the ARGUE corpus, an annotated collection of 109,553 forum posts (11,216 discussion threads) from the debate website 4forums.com. On 4forums, a person starts a discussion by posting a topic or a question in a particular category, such as society, politics, or religion. Some example topics can be seen in Table 1. Forum participants can then post their opinions, choosing whether to respond directly to a previous post or to the top level topic (start a new thread). These discussions are essentially dialogic; however the affordances of the forum such as asynchrony, and the ability to start a new thread rather than continue an existing one, leads to dialogic structures that are different than other multiparty informal conversations (Fox Tree, 2010). An additional source of dialogic structure in these discussions, above and beyond the thread structure, is the use of the quote mechanism, in which participants often break a previous post down into the components of its argument and respond to each component in turn. Many posts include quotations of previous posts. Because we hypothesize that these posts are more targeted at a particular proposition that the poster wants to comment on, than posts and replies in general, we focus here on understanding the relationship between a quoted text and a response, and the linguistic reflexes of those relationships. Examples of quote/response pairs for several of our topics are provided in Figure 1.

The most similar work to our own is that of Wang & Rose (2010) who analyzed Usenet forum quote/response structures. This work did not distinguish agreement vs. disagreement across quote/response pairs. Rather they show that they can use a variant of LSA to improve accuracy for identifying a parent post, given a response post, with 70% accuracy. Other similar work uses Congressional debate transcripts or blogs or other social media to develop methods for distinguishing agreement from disagreement or to distinguish rebuttals from out-of-context posts (Thomas et al., 2006; Bansal et al., 2008; Awadallah et al., 2010; Walker et al., ; Burfoot, 2008; Mishne and Glance, 2006; Popescu and Pennacchiotti, 2010). These methods are directly applicable, but the genre of the language is so different from our informal forums that the results are not directly comparable. Work by Somasundaran & Wiebe (2009, 2010) has examined debate websites and focused on automatically determining the stance of a debate participant with respect to a particular issue. This work has treated each post as a text to be classified in terms of stance, for a particular topic, and shown that discourse relations such as concessions and the identification of argumentation triggers improves performance . Their work, along with others, also indicates that for such tasks it is difficult to beat a unigram baseline (Pang and Lee, 2008). Other work has focused on the social network structure of online forums (Murakami and Raymond, 2010; Agrawal et al., 2003). However, Agarwal's work assumed that adjacent posts always disagree, and did not use any of the information in the text. Murakami & Raymond (2010) show that simple rules defined on the textual content of the post can improve over Agarwal's results.

Section 2 discusses our corpus in more detail, describes how we collected annotations using Mechanical Turk, and presents results of a corpus analysis of the use of particular discourse cues. Section 3 describes how we set up classification experiments for distinguishing agreement from disagreement, and Section 4 presents our results for agreement classification. We also characterize the linguistic reflexes of this relation. We analyze the utility of meta-post features, contextual features, dependency features and word-based features for signaling the disagreement relation. We show that using contextual and dialogic features we can achieve accuracies up to 68% as compared to a unigram baseline of 63%.

2 Data and Corpus Analysis

Table 1 provides an overview of some of the characteristics of our corpus by topic. Figure 2 shows the wording of the survey questions that we posted for each quote/response as Mechanical Turk hits.

Topic	Discs	Posts	NumA	P/A	A>1P	PL	Agree	Sarcasm	Emote	Attack	Nasty
evolution	872	10292	580	17.74	76%	576	10%	6%	16%	13%	9%
gun control	825	7968	411	19.39	66%	521	11%	8%	21%	16%	12%
abortion	564	7354	574	12.81	69 %	454	9%	6%	31%	16%	12%
gay marriage	305	3586	342	10.49	69%	522	13%	9%	23%	12%	8%
existence of God	105	1581	258	6.13	66%	569	11 %	7%	26%	14%	10%
healthcare	81	702	112	6.27	64%	522	14%	10%	34%	17%	17%
communism vs. capitalism	38	585	110	5.32	59%	393	23%	8%	15%	8%	0%
death penalty	25	500	138	3.62	62%	466	25%	5%	5%	5%	5%
climate change	40	361	116	3.11	55%	375	20%	9%	17%	26%	17%
marijuana legalization	13	160	72	2.22	38%	473	5%	2%	20%	5%	5%

Table 1: Characteristics of Different Topics. **KEY**: Number of discussions and posts on the topic (**Discs, Posts**). Number of authors (**NumA**). Posts per author (**P/A**). Authors with more than one post (**A > 1P**). Median post Length in Characters (**PL**). The remainder of the columns are the annotations shown in Figure 2. Percentage of posts that agree (**Agree%**), use sarcasm (**Sarcasm%**), are emotional (**Emote**), attack the previous poster (**Attack**), and are nasty (**Nasty**). The scalar values are threshholded at -1,1.

Our corpus is derived from a debate oriented internet forum called 4forums.com. It is a typical internet forum built on the vBulletin software. People initiate discussions (threads) and respond to others' posts. Each thread has a tree-like dialogue structure. Each post has author information and a timestamp with minute resolution. Many posts include quotations of previous posts. For this work we chose to focus on quotations because they establish a clear relationship between the quoted text and the response.

Our corpus consists of 11,216 discussions and 109,553 posts by 2764 authors. We hand annotated discussions for topic from a set of previously identified contentious political and social issues. The website is tailored to a US audience and our topics are somewhat US centric. Table 1 describes features of our topics in order of decreasing discussion count. When restricted to these topics, the corpus consists of 2868 discussions, 33,089 posts, and 1302 authors.

Many posts include quotations. Overall 60,382 posts contain one or more quotation. Within our topics of interest, nearly 20,000 posts contain quotations. We defined a quote-response pair (Q-R pair) where the response was the portion of the responding post directly following a quotation but preceding any additional quotations.

We selected 10,003 Q-R pairs from the topics of interest for a Mechanical Turk annotation task. These were biased by cue word to ensure adequate data for discourse marker analysis (See Section 2.1. For this task we showed annotators seven Q-R pairs and asked them to judge Agreement/Disagreement and a set of other measures as shown in Figure 2. Most of our measures were scalar; we chose to do this because previous work on estimating the relationship between MTurk annotations and expert annotations suggest that taking the means of scalar annotations could be a good way to reduce noise in MTurk annotations (Snow et al., 2008). For all of the measures annotated, the Turkers were not given additional definitions of their meaning. For example, we let Turkers to use their native intuitions about what it means for a post to be sarcastic, since previous work suggests that non-specialists tend to collapse all forms of verbal irony under the term sarcastic (Bryant and Fox Tree, 2002). We did not ask Turkers to distinguish between sarcasm and other forms of verbal irony such as hyperbole, understatement, rhetorical questions and jocularity (Gibbs, 2000).

Agreement was a scalar judgment on an 11 point scale [-5,5] implemented with a slider. The annotators were also able to signal uncertainty with an CAN'T TELL option. Each of the pairs was annotated by 5-7 annotators. We showed the first 155 characters of each quote and each response. We also provided a SHOW MORE button which expanded the post to its full length. After annotation, we removed a number of Q-R pairs in cases where a clear link between the quote and a previous post could not be established, e.g. the source quoted was not another post, but the NY Times. This left us with 8,242 Q-R pairs for our final analysis. Resampling to a natural distribution left us with 2,847 pairs which we used to build our machine learning test set. We used the remaining annotated and unannotated pairs for development.

Type	α	Survey Question
S	0.62	**Agree/Disagree**: Does the respondent agree or disagree with the prior post?
S	0.32	**Fact/Emotion**: Is the respondent attempting to make a fact based argument or appealing to feelings and emotions?
S	0.42	**Attack/Insult**: Is the respondent being supportive/respectful or are they attacking/insulting in their writing?
B	0.22	**Sarcasm**: Is the respondent using sarcasm?
S	0.46	**Nice/Nasty**: Is the respondent attempting to be nice or is their attitude fairly nasty?

Figure 2: Mechanical Turk Annotations (Binary = B and Scalar = S) and level of agreement as Krippendorff's α.

Figure 3 provides examples from the end points and means of the annotations for three of the questions, Respect/Insult, Sarcasm, and Fact/Emotion. Nice/Nasty and Respect/Insult are strongly correlated by worker annotations $r(54003) = 0.84$, $p < 2.2\text{e-}16$ and both weakly correlated with Agree/Disagree ratings ($r(54003) = 0.32$ and $r(54003)=0.36$, respectively; $p < 2.2\text{e-}16$) and Fact/Emotion ratings ($r(54003) = 0.32$ and $r(54003)=0.31$, respectively; $p < 2.2\text{e-}16$), while Agree/Disagree and Fact/Emotion ratings show the smallest correlation, $r(54003)=0.11$, $p < 2.2\text{e-}16$. For the linguistic marker correlations discussed below we averaged scores across annotators, a process which sharpened correlations (e.g., Respect/Insult means correlate with Agree/Disagree means more strongly ($r(5393) = 0.51$) as well as Nice/Nasty means ($r(5393) = 0.91$; Agree/Disagree is far less correlated with Fact/Emotion ($r(5393) = 0.07$). Interannotator agreement was computed using Krippendorff's α (due to the variability in number of annotators that completed each hit), assuming an ordinal scale for all measures except sarcasm; see Figure 2. The low agreement for Sarcasm accords with native intuition – it is the class with the least dependence on lexicalization and the most subject to inter-speaker stylistic variation. The relatively low results for Fact/Emotion is perhaps due to the emotional charge many ideological arguments engender; informal examination of posts that showed the most disagreement in this category often showed a cutting comment or a snide remark at the end of a post, which was was ignored by some annotators and evidence for others (one Emotional post in Figure 3 is clearly an insult, but was uniformly labeled as -5 by all annotators).

2.1 Discourse Markers

Both psychological research on discourse processes (Fox Tree and Schrock, 1999; Fox Tree and Schrock, 2002; Groen et al., 2010) and computational work on agreement (Galley et al., 2004) indicate that discourse markers are strongly associated with particular pragmatic functions. Because of their salient position, we test the role of turn-initial markers in predicting upcoming content (Fox Tree and Schrock, 2002; Groen et al., 2010). Based on manual inspection of a subset of the corpus, we constructed a list of 20 discourse markers; 17 of these occurred at least 50 times in a quote response (upper bound of 700 samples): *actually, and, because, but, I believe, I know, I see, I think, just, no, oh, really, so, well, yes, you know, you mean*. All of their occurrences became part of the 10,003 Q-R pairs annotated.

The top discourse markers highlighting disagreement were *really* (67% read a response beginning with this marker as prefacing a disagreement with a prior post), *no* (66%), *actually* (60%), *but* (58%), *so* (58%), and *you mean* (57%). At this point, the next most disagreeable category was the unmarked category, with about 50% of respondents interpreting an unmarked post as disagreeing. On the other hand, the most agreeable marker was *yes* (73% read a response beginning with this marker as prefacing an agreement) followed by *I know* (64%), *I believe* (62%), *I think* (61%), and *just* (57%). The other markers were close to the unmarked category: *and* (50%), *because* (51%), *oh* (51%), *I see* (52%), *you know* (54%), and *well* (55%).

The overall agreement on sarcasm was low, as in other computational work on recognizing sarcasm (Davidov et al., 2010). At most, only 31% of respondents agreed that the material after a discourse marker was sarcastic, with the most sarcastic markers being *you mean* (31%), *oh* (29%), *really* (24%), *so* (22%), and *I see* (21%). Only 15% of respondents rated the unmarked category as sarcastic (e.g., fewer than 1 out of 6 respondents). The cues *I think* (10%), *I believe* (9%), and *actually* (10%) were the least sarcastic markers.

Taken together, these ratings suggest that the cues *really*, *you mean*, and *so* can be used to indicate both

Class	Very High Degree	Neutral	Very Low Degree
Insult or Attack	Well, you have proven yoruself to be a man with no brain, that is for sure. The definition that was given was the one that scientists use, not the layperson.	The empire you defend is tyrannical. They are responsible for the death of millions.	Very well put.
	Is that what you said right before they started banning assault weapons?...Obviously, you're gullible. Since you're such a brainiac and all, why don't you visit the UN website and see what your beloved UN is up to?	Bad comparisons. A fair comparison would be comparing the total number of defensive gun uses to the total number of gun crimes (not just limiting it to gun homicides).	In some cases yes, in others no. If the mutation gives a huge advantage, then there will be a decline in the size of the gene pool for a while (eg when the Australian rabbit population...
Sarcasm	My pursuit of happiness is denied by trees existing. Let's burn them down and destroy the environment. It's much better than me being unhappy.	An interesting analysis of that article you keep quoting from the World Net Daily [url]	I would suggest you look at the faero island mouse then. That is a new species, and it is not man doing it, but rather nature itself.
	Like the crazy idea the Earth goes around the Sun.	Indeed there is no diffrence it is still a dead baby but throwing a baby in a trash can and leaving it for dead is far more cruel than abortion.	Too late, drug usage has already created those epidemics. Legalizing drugs may increase some of them temporarily, but they already exist.
Emotion-based Argument	Really! You can prove that most prolifers don't care about women?...it is idiotic thinking like this that makes me respect you less and less.	Fine by me. First, I don't consider having a marriage recognized by government to be a "right". Second, I've said many times I don't think government should be in the marriage business at all.	Sure. Here is an explanation. The 14C Method. That is from the Radiocarbon WEB info site by the Waikato Radiocarbon Dating Lab of the University of Waikato (New Zeland).
	I love Jesus John the Beloved is my most favorite writer throughout time If you think I have a problem with a follower of Jesus your wrong. I have a problem with the Christians	I agree that the will to survive is an amazing phenomenon when put to the test. But I do not agree with your statement of life at *any* cost. There will always be a time when the humane/loving thing to do is to let an infant/child/adult go.	Heller is about determining the answer to a long standing question on the nature of the Second Amendment, and how much gun control is legally allowed. Roe v. Wade is about finding legal precedent for the murder of unborn children. I see absolutely no comparison between the two.

Figure 3: Sample Responses for the Insult, Sarcasm, and Fact/Feeling spectrums

disagreement and sarcasm. However, *but*, *no*, and *actually* can be used for disagreement, but not sarcasm. And *I know* (14% sarcastic, similar to None), *I believe*, and *I think* can be used for non-sarcastic agreement.

From informal analyses, we hypothesized that *really* and *oh* might indicate sarcasm. While we found evidence supporting this for *really*, it was not the case for *oh*. Instead, *oh* was used to indicate emotion; it was the discourse marker with the highest ratings of feeling over fact.

Despite the fact that it would seem that disagreement would be positively correlated with sarcasm, disagreement and sarcasm were not related. There were two tests possible. One tested the percentage of people who identified an item as disagreeing against the percentage of people who identified it as sarcasm, $r(16) = -.27$, $p = .27$ (tested on 17 discourse markers plus the None category). The other tested the degree of disagreement (from -5 to +5) against the percentage of people who identified the post as sarcastic, $r(16) = -.33$, $p = .18$.

However, we did observe relationships between sarcasm and other variables. Two results support the argument that sarcasm is emotional and personal. The more sarcastic, the nastier (rather than nicer), $r(16) = .87$, $p < .001$. In addition, the more sarcastic, the more emotional (over factual) respondents were judged to be, $r(16) = .62$, $p = .006$ Taken together, these analyses suggest that sarcasm is emotional and personal, but not necessarily a sign of disagreement.

3 Machine Learning Experimental Setup

For our experiments we used the Weka machine learning toolkit. All results are from 10 fold cross-validation on a balanced test set. Unless otherwise mentioned, we used thresholds of 1 and -1 on the mean agreement judgment to determine agreement and disagreement respectively. We omitted those Q-R pairs which were judged neutral (mean annotator judgment in the (-1,1) range).

As described above, from the original 10,003 Q-R pairs we applied certain constraints (notably requirement that we be able to identify the originating post) which left us with 8,242. We then resampled to obtain a natural distribution leaving us with 2,847 pairs. Applying the (-1,1) threshold and balancing the result yielded a test set of 682 Q-R pairs.

3.1 Classifiers

Our experiments used two simple classifiers: NaiveBayes and JRip. NaiveBayes makes a strict independence assumption and can be swamped by the sheer number of features we used, but it is a solid baseline and does a decent job of suggesting which features are more powerful. JRip is a rule based classifier which produces a compact model suitable for human consumption and quick application. JRip is not without its own limitations but, for our task, it shows better results than NaiveBayes. The model it builds uses only a handful of features.

3.2 Feature Extraction

Our aim was to develop features for the automatic identification of agreement and disagreement that would do well on the task and provide useful baselines for comparisons with previous and future work. Features are grouped into sets as shown in Table 2 and discussed in more detail below.

Set	Description/Examples
MetaPost	Non-lexical features. E.g. posterid, time between posts, etc.
Unigrams, Bigrams	Word and Word Pair frequencies
Cue Words	Initial unigram, bigram, and trigram
Punctuation	Collapsed into one of the following: ??, !!, ?!
LIWC	LIWC measures and frequencies
Dependencies	Dependencies derived from the Stanford Parser.
Generalized Dependencies	Dependency features generalized with respect to POS of the head word and opinion polarity of both words.

Table 2: Feature Sets, Descriptions, and Examples

Unigrams, Bigrams, Trigrams. Results of previous work suggest that a unigram baseline can be difficult to beat for certain types of debates (Walker et al., ; Somasundaran and Wiebe, 2010). Thus we derived both unigrams and bigrams as features. We captured the final token as a feature by padding with -nil- tokens when building the bigrams. See below for comments on initial uni/bi/tri-grams.

MetaPost Info. Previous work suggested that non-lexical features like poster ids and the time between posts might contain indicators of disagreement. People on these forums get to know one another and often enjoy repeatedly arguing with the same person. In addition, we hypothesized that the "heat" of a particular conversation could be correlated with rapid-fire exchanges, as indicated by short time periods between posts.

Thus these features involve structure outside of the quote/response text. This includes author information, time between posts, the $\log_{10}$ of the time between posts, the number of other quotes in the response, whether the quote responds to a post by the response's author, the percent of the quoted post which is actually quoted, whether the quoted post is by the same author as the response (there were only an handful of these), whether the response mentions the quote author by name, and whether the response is longer than the quote.

The forum software effectively does this annotation for us so there is no reason not to consider it as a clue in our quest to understand and interpret online dialogue.

Discourse Markers. Previous work on dialogue analysis has repeatedly noted the discourse functions of particular discourse markers, and our corpus analysis above also suggests their use in this particular dataset (Hirschberg and Litman, 1993; Fox Tree, 2010; Schiffrin, 1987; Di Eugenio et al., 1997; Moser and Moore, 1995). However, because discourse markers can be stacked up *Oh, so really* we decided to represent this feature as post initial unigrams, bigrams and trigrams.

Repeated Punctuation. Informal analyses of our data suggested that repeated sequential use of particular types of punctuation such as **!!** and **??** did not mean the same thing as simple counts or frequencies of punctuation across a whole post. Thus we developed distinct features for a subset of these repetitions.

LIWC. We also derived features using the Linguistics Inquiry Word Count tool (LIWC-2001) (Pennebaker et al., 2001). LIWC classifies words into 69 categories and counts how many words get classified into each category. Some LIWC features that we expect to be important are words per sentence (WPS), pronominal forms, and positive and negative emotion words.

Dependency and Generalized Dependency. We used the Stanford parser to extract dependency features for each quote and response (De Marneffe et al., 2006; Klein and Manning, 2003). The dependency parse for a given sentence is a set of triples, composed of a grammatical relation and the pair of words for which the grammatical relation holds (rel_i, w_j, w_k), where rel_i is the dependency relation among words w_j and w_k. The word w_j is the HEAD of the dependency relation.

Following (Joshi and Penstein-Rosé, 2009) we extracted generalized dependency features by leaving one dependency element lexicalized and generalizing the other to part of speech. Joshi & Rose's results suggested that this approach would work better than either fully lexicalized or fully generalized dependency features.

Opinion Dependencies. Somasundaran & Wiebe (2009) introduce the concept of features that identify the TARGET of opinion words. Inspired by this approach, we used the MPQA dictionary of opinion words to select the subset of dependency and generalized dependency features in which those opinion words appear. For these features we replace the opinion words with their positive or negative polarity equivalents.

Cosine Similarity. This feature is based on previous work on threading. We derive cosine-similarity measure using tf-idf vectors where the document frequency was derived from the entire topic restricted corpus.

Annotations. We also add features representing information that we do not currently derive automatically, but which might be automatically derived in future work based on annotations in the corpus. These include the topic and Mechanical Turk annotations for Fact/Emotion, Respect/Insult, Sarcasm, and Nasty/Nice, which could reasonably be expected to be recognized independently of Agreement/Disagreement.

Feature type	**Selected Features**
Meta	number-of-other-quotes, percent-quoted, author-quote-USERNAME
Initial n-gram	*yes, so, I agree, well said, really?, I don't know*
Bigram	*that you, ? -nil-, you have, evolution is*
Dependency	dep-nsubj(agree, i), dep-nsubj(think, you), dep-prep-with(agree, you)
Opinion Dependency	dep-opinion-nsubj(negative, you), dep-opinion-dep(proven, negative), dep-opinion-aux(positive, to)
Annotations	topic-gay marriage, mean-response-nicenasty, mean-unsure-sarcasm

Table 3: Some of the more useful features for each category, using χ^2 for feature selection.

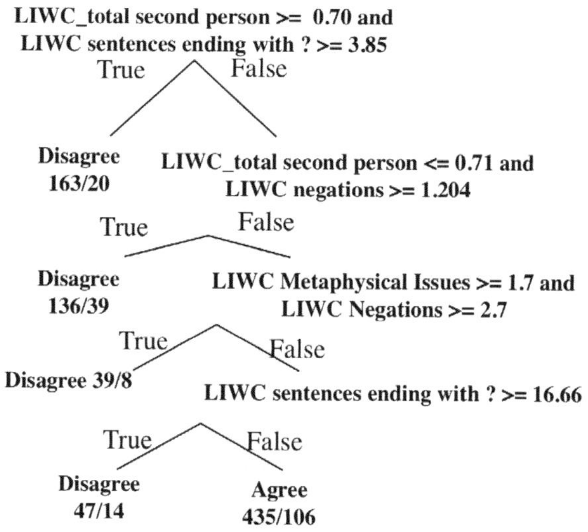

Figure 4: Sample model learned using JRip. The numbers represent (total instances covered by a rule / number incorrectly labeled). This particular model was built on development data.

4 Results

Table 3 shows features which were selected for each of our feature categories using a χ^2 test for feature selection. These results vindicate our interest in discourse markers as cues to argument structure, as well as the importance of the generalized dependency features and opinion target pairs (Wang and Rosé, 2010; Somasundaran and Wiebe, 2009). Figure 4 shows a sample model learned using JRip.

We limit our pair-wise comparisons between classifiers and feature sets to those corresponding to par-

Feats	NB	JRipχ^2
Uni,UniCue	0.578	0.626
BOW	0.598	0.654
Meta	0.579	0.588
Response Local	0.600	0.666
Quote Local	0.531	0.588
Both Local	0.601	**0.682**
Meta+Local	0.603	0.654
All	0.603	0.632
Just Annotations	0.765	0.814
All+Annotations	0.603	0.795

Table 4: Accuracies on a balanced test set (random baseline: 0.5). NB = NaiveBayes. JRipχ^2 = Jripper with χ^2 feature selection on the training set during cross validation. **BOW** = Unigrams, CueWords, Bigrams, Trigrams, LIWC, Repeated Punctuation. **Response/Quote/Both Local** uses only those features which exist in the text of the response or quote respectively. It consists of LIWC, dependencies, generalized dependencies, the various n-grams, and length measures.

ticular hypotheses. We conducted five tests with Bonferroni correction to .01 for a .05 level of significance.

While we hypothesized that more sophisticated linguistic features would improve over unigram features alone, a paired t-test using the results in Table 4 indicate that there is no statistical difference between the performance of JRip using only response local features (JRip,ResponseLocal), as compared to the Unigram,UniCue features ($t(9)$ = 2.18, p = .06).

However, a paired t-test using the results in Table 4 indicate that there is a statistical difference between the performance of JRip using local features from both the quote and the response, (JRip,BothLocal) as compared to the Unigram,UniCue features ($t(9)$ = 3.94, p =.003). This shows that the contextual features do matter, even though (JRip,BothLocal) does **not** provide significant improvements over (JRip,Response Local) ($t(9)$ = .92, p = .38).

In general, examination of the table suggests that the JRip classifier performs better than Naive Bayes. A paired t-test indicates that there is a statistical difference between the performance of JRip using local features from both the quote and the response, (JRip,BothLocal) (JRip,BothLocal) and Naive Bayes using local features from both the quote and the response, (NB,BothLocal) ($t(9)$ = 3.43, p = .007).

In addition, with an eye toward the future, we examined whether automatic recognition of sarcasm, attack/insult, fact/feeling nice/nasty could possibly improve results for recognizing disagreement. Using the human annotations as a proxy for automatic results, we get classification accuracies of over 81% (JRip,JustAnnotations). This suggests it might be possible to improve results over our best current results (JRip,BothLocal) ($t(9)$ = 6.09, $p < .001$).

Another interesting fact, is that despite its use in previous work for threading, the cosine similarity between the quote and response did not improve accuracy for the classifiers we tested, over and above the use of text-based contextual features. Further investigation is required to draw conclusions about this or similar metrics (LSA, PMI, etc.).

5 Discussion and Conclusion

In this paper, we have introduced a new collection of internet forum posts, the ARGUE corpus, collected across a range of ideological topics, and containing scalar Agreement/Disagreement annotations over quote-response pairs within a post. We have demonstrated that we can achieve a significant improvement over a unigram baseline agreement detection system using features from both a response and the quote being responded to.

Beyond agreement, the ARGUE corpus contains finer-grained annotations for degrees of insult, nastiness, and emotional appeal, as well as the presence of sarcasm. We have demonstrated that these classes (especially insult and nastiness) correlate with agreement. While the utility of these classes as features for agreement detection is dependent on how easily they are learned, in closing we note that they also afford us a richer understanding of how argumentative conversation flows. In section 2.1.2, we outlined how they can yield understanding of the potential functions of a discourse particle within a particular post. They may as allow us to understand the extent to which participants react in kind, rewarding insult with insult or kindness in turn. In future work, we hope to turn to these conversational dynamics.

In future work, it would be useful to build a ternary classifier which labels

Agree/Disagree/Neutral, thus reflecting the true distribution of these dialogue acts in the data. Additionally, the proportion of agreeing utterances varies widely across media so it may be desirable to add an appropriate prior when adapting the model to a new dataset.

Acknowledgments

This work was funded by Grant NPS-BAA-03 to UCSC and and through the Intelligence Advanced Research Projects Activity (IARPA) through the Army Research Laboratory. We'd like to thank Craig Martell for helpful discussions over the course of this project, and the anonymous reviewers for useful feedback. We would also like to thank Michael Minor and Jason Aumiller for their contributions to scripting and the database.

References

R. Agrawal, S. Rajagopalan, R. Srikant, and Y. Xu. 2003. Mining newsgroups using networks arising from social behavior. In *Proceedings of the 12th international conference on World Wide Web*, pages 529–535. ACM.

J.L. Austin. 1965. *How to do things with words*. Oxford University Press, New York.

R. Awadallah, M. Ramanath, and G. Weikum. 2010. Language-model-based pro/con classification of political text. In *Proceeding of the 33rd international ACM SIGIR conference on Research and development in information retrieval*, pages 747–748. ACM.

M. Bansal, C. Cardie, and L. Lee. 2008. The power of negative thinking: Exploiting label disagreement in the min-cut classification framework. *Proceedings of COLING: Companion volume: Posters*, pages 13–16.

J. Bollen, H. Mao, and X. Zeng. 2011. Twitter mood predicts the stock market. *Journal of Computational Science*.

G.A. Bryant and J.E. Fox Tree. 2002. Recognizing verbal irony in spontaneous speech. *Metaphor and symbol*, 17(2):99–119.

C. Burfoot. 2008. Using multiple sources of agreement information for sentiment classification of political transcripts. In *Australasian Language Technology Association Workshop 2008*, volume 6, pages 11–18.

Robert B. Cialdini. 2000. *Influence: Science and Practice (4th Edition)*. Allyn & Bacon.

D. Davidov, O. Tsur, and A. Rappoport. 2010. Semi-supervised recognition of sarcastic sentences in twitter and amazon. In *Proceedings of the Fourteenth Conference on Computational Natural Language Learning*, pages 107–116. Association for Computational Linguistics.

M.C. De Marneffe, B. MacCartney, and C.D. Manning. 2006. Generating typed dependency parses from phrase structure parses. In *Proceedings of LREC*, volume 6, pages 449–454. Citeseer.

Barbara Di Eugenio, Johanna D. Moore, and Massimo Paolucci. 1997. Learning features that predict cue usage. In *Proceedings of the 35th Annual Meeting of the Association for Computational Linguistics, ACL/EACL 97*, pages 80–87.

J.E. Fox Tree and J.C. Schrock. 1999. Discourse Markers in Spontaneous Speech: Oh What a Difference an Oh Makes. *Journal of Memory and Language*, 40(2):280–295.

J.E. Fox Tree and J.C. Schrock. 2002. Basic meanings of you know and I mean. *Journal of Pragmatics*, 34(6):727–747.

J. E. Fox Tree. 2010. Discourse markers across speakers and settings. *Language and Linguistics Compass*, 3(1):113.

M. Galley, K. McKeown, J. Hirschberg, and E. Shriberg. 2004. Identifying agreement and disagreement in conversational speech: Use of bayesian networks to model pragmatic dependencies. In *Proceedings of the 42nd Annual Meeting on Association for Computational Linguistics*, pages 669–es. Association for Computational Linguistics.

R.W. Gibbs. 2000. Irony in talk among friends. *Metaphor and Symbol*, 15(1):5–27.

M. Groen, J. Noyes, and F. Verstraten. 2010. The Effect of Substituting Discourse Markers on Their Role in Dialogue. *Discourse Processes: A Multidisciplinary Journal*, 47(5):33.

Julia Hirschberg and Diane Litman. 1993. Empirical studies on the disambiguation of cue phrases. *Computational Linguistics*, 19(3):501–530.

John E. Hunter. 1987. A model of compliance-gaining message selection. *Communication Monographs*, 54(1):54–63.

M. Joshi and C. Penstein-Rosé. 2009. Generalizing dependency features for opinion mining. In *Proceedings of the ACL-IJCNLP 2009 Conference Short Papers*, pages 313–316. Association for Computational Linguistics.

D. Klein and C.D. Manning. 2003. Accurate unlexicalized parsing. In *Proceedings of the 41st Annual Meeting on Association for Computational Linguistics-Volume 1*, pages 423–430. Association for Computational Linguistics.

G. Mishne and N. Glance. 2006. Leave a reply: An analysis of weblog comments. In *Third annual workshop on the Weblogging ecosystem*. Citeseer.

Margaret G. Moser and Johanna Moore. 1995. Investigating cue selection and placement in tutorial discourse. In *ACL 95*, pages 130–137.

A. Murakami and R. Raymond. 2010. Support or Oppose? Classifying Positions in Online Debates from Reply Activities and Opinion Expressions. In *Proceedings of the 23rd International Conference on Computational Linguistics: Posters*, pages 869–875. Association for Computational Linguistics.

B. Pang and L. Lee. 2008. Opinion mining and sentiment analysis. *Foundations and Trends in Information Retrieval*, 2(1-2):1–135.

J. W. Pennebaker, L. E. Francis, and R. J. Booth, 2001. *LIWC: Linguistic Inquiry and Word Count.*

A.M. Popescu and M. Pennacchiotti. 2010. Detecting controversial events from twitter. In *Proceedings of the 19th ACM international conference on Information and knowledge management*, pages 1873–1876. ACM.

Deborah Schiffrin. 1987. *Discourse Markers*. Cambridge University Press, Cambridge, U.K.

R. Snow, B. O'Connor, D. Jurafsky, and A.Y. Ng. 2008. Cheap and fast—but is it good?: evaluating non-expert annotations for natural language tasks. In *Proceedings of the Conference on Empirical Methods in Natural Language Processing*, pages 254–263. Association for Computational Linguistics.

S. Somasundaran and J. Wiebe. 2009. Recognizing stances in online debates. In *Proceedings of the Joint Conference of the 47th Annual Meeting of the ACL and the 4th International Joint Conference on Natural Language Processing of the AFNLP: Volume 1-Volume 1*, pages 226–234. Association for Computational Linguistics.

S. Somasundaran and J. Wiebe. 2010. Recognizing stances in ideological on-line debates. In *Proceedings of the NAACL HLT 2010 Workshop on Computational Approaches to Analysis and Generation of Emotion in Text*, pages 116–124. Association for Computational Linguistics.

M. Thomas, B. Pang, and L. Lee. 2006. Get out the vote: Determining support or opposition from Congressional floor-debate transcripts. In *Proceedings of the 2006 conference on empirical methods in natural language processing*, pages 327–335. Association for Computational Linguistics.

Marilyn Walker, Rob Abbott, Pranav Anand, Jean E. Fox Tree, Robeson Bowmani, and Michael Minor. Cats Rule and Dogs Drool: Classifying Stance in Online Debate.

Y.C. Wang and C.P. Rosé. 2010. Making conversational structure explicit: identification of initiation-response pairs within online discussions. In *Human Language Technologies: The 2010 Annual Conference of the North American Chapter of the Association for Computational Linguistics*, pages 673–676. Association for Computational Linguistics.

What pushes their buttons? Predicting comment polarity from the content of political blog posts

Ramnath Balasubramanyan
Language Technologies Institute
Carnegie Mellon University
rbalasub@cs.cmu.edu

William W. Cohen
Machine Learning Department
Carnegie Mellon University
wcohen@cs.cmu.edu

Doug Pierce and **David P. Redlawsk**
Political Science Department
Rutgers University
drpierce@eden.rutgers.edu, redlawsk@rutgers.edu

Abstract

Political blogs as a form of social media allow for an uniquely interactive form of political discourse. This is especially evident in focused blogs with a strong ideological identity. We investigate techniques to identify topics within the context of the community, which when discussed in a blog post evoke a discernible positive or negative collective opinion from readers who respond to posts in comments. This is done by using computational methods to assign sentiment polarity to blog comments and learning community specific models that summarize issues tackled by blogs and predict the polarity based on the topics discussed in a blog post.

1 Introduction

Recent work in political psychology has made it clear that political decision-making is strongly influenced by emotion. For instance, (Lodge and Taber, 2000) propose a theory of "motivated reasoning", in which political information is processed in a way that is determined, in part, by a quickly-computed emotional react to that information. Strong experimental evidence for motivated reasoning (sometimes called "hot cognition") exists (Huang and Price, 2001); (Redlawsk, 2002); (Redlawsk, 2006); (Isbell et al., 2006). However, despite some recent proposals (Kim et al., 2008) it is unclear how to computationally model a person's emotional reaction to news, and how to collect the data necessary to fit such a model. One problem is that emotional reactions are different for different people - a fact exploited in the use of political "code words" intended to invoke a reaction in only a particular subset of the electorate (a technique sometimes called "dog whistle politics").

In this paper, we evaluate the use of machine learning methods to predict how *members of a specific political community will emotionally reaction to different types of news*. More specifically, we use a dataset of widely read ("A-list") political blogs, and attempt to predict the aggregate sentiment in the comment section of blogs, as a function of the textual content of the blog posting. In this paper, we consider only predicting polarity (positive and negative feeling). In contrast to work done traditionally in sentiment analysis which focuses on determining the sentiment expressed in text, in this work, we focus on the task of predicting the sentiment that a block of text will evoke in readers, expressed in the comment section, as a response to the blog post.

This task is related to, but distinct from, several other studies that have been made using comments and discussions in political communities, or analysis of sentiment in comments - (Yano et al., 2009), (O'Connor et al., 2010), (Tumasjan et al., 2010). Below we discuss the methods used to address the various parts of this task. First, we evaluate two methods to automatically determine the comment polarity: SentiWordNet (Baccianella and Sebastiani, 2010) a general purpose resource that assigns sentiment scores to entries in WordNet, and an automated corpus-specific technique based on pointwise mutual information. The quality of the polarity assessments by these techniques are made by comparing them to hand annotated assessments on a small number of blog posts. Second, we consider two methods for predicting comment polarity from post content: support vector machine classification, and sLDA, a topic-modeling-based approach. Finally, we demonstrate that emotional reactions are indeed community-specific, compare the accuracy of this approach to the more traditional approach of predicting sentiment of a text from the text itself, and present our conclusions.

2 Data

In this study, we use a collection of blog posts from five blogs: Carpetbagger(CB)[1], Daily Kos(DK)[2], Matthew Yglesias(MY)[3], Red State(RS)[4], and Right Wing News(RWN)[5], that focus on American politics made available by (Yano et al., 2009). The posts were collected during November 2007 to October 2008, which preceded the US presidential elections held in November 2008. The blogs included in the dataset vary in political idealogy with blogs like Daily Kos that are Democrat-leaning and blogs like Red State tending to be much more conservative. Since we are interested in studying the responses to blog posts, the corpus only contains posts where there have been at least one comment in the six days after the post was published. It is important to note that only the text in the blog posts and comments are used in this study. All non-textual information like pictures, hyperlinks, videos etc. are discarded. In terms of text processing, for each blog, a vocabulary is created consisting of all terms that occur at least 5 times in the blog. Stopwords are eliminated using a standard stopword list. Each blog post is then represented as a bag of words from the post. Table 2 shows statistics of the datasets. Each dataset is studied separately for the most part in the rest of the paper.

[1]http://www.thecarpetbaggerreport.com

[2]http://www.dailykos.com/

[3]http://yglesias.thinkprogress.org/

[4]http://www.redstate.com/

[5]http://rightwingnews.com/

3 Labelling comments with sentiment polarity

The first step in understanding the nature of posts that evoke emotional responses is to get a measure of the polarity in the sentiment expressed in the comments section of a blog post. The measure indicates the ability of the issues in the blog post and its treatment, to evoke strong emotions in readers.

3.1 SentiWordNet

In the first stage of the study, we use SentiWordNet (Baccianella and Sebastiani, 2010) which associates a large number of words in WordNet with a positive, negative and objective score (summing up to 1). Firstly, all the comments for a blog post in the comment section are aggregated and for the words in the comments that are found in SentiWordNet, the net positive and negative scores are computed. Since SentiWordNet entries are associated with word senses and because we don't perform word sense disambiguation, the SentiWordNet polarity of the most dominant word sense is used for words in the comment section. The sentiment in the comment section is deemed to be positive if the net positive score exceeds the negative score and negative otherwise. Therefore, each blog post is now associated with a binary response variable indicating the polarity of the sentiment expressed in the comments.

3.2 Using pointwise mutual information

A second technique to determine the sentiment polarity of comments uses the principle of pointwise mutual information (PMI)(Turney, 2002). We first construct a seed list of positive and negative words by choosing the 100 topmost positive and negative words from SentiWordNet and manually eliminating words from this list that don't pertain to sentiment in our context. (Appendix A has the list of seed words used.) This seed list is used to construct a larger set of positive and negative words by computing the PMI of the words in the seed lists with every other word in the vocabulary. It's important to note that this list is constructed for the specific corpus that we work with. Because every blog is processed separately, we construct a different sentiment word list for each blog based on the statistics

Blog	Pol alignment	#posts	Vocabulary size	Avg #words per post	Avg #comments per post	Avg #words per comment section
Carpetbagger (CB)	liberal	1201	4998	170	31	1306
Daily Kos (DK)	liberal	2597	6400	103	198	3883
Matthew Yglesias (MY)	liberal	1813	4010	69	35	1420
Red State (RS)	conservative	2357	8029	158	28	806
Right Wing Nation (RWN)	conservative	1184	6205	185	33	1015

Table 1: Dataset statistics

of word occurences. Words in the vocabulary are ranked by the difference in the average of the PMI with positive and negative seed words. The top 1000 words in the resultant sorted list are treated as positive words and the bottom 1000 words as negative words. The comment section of every post is tagged with a positive or negative polarity as in the previous section by computing the total positive and negative word counts.

Using the same seed word list, the procedure is performed separately for each blog resulting in sentiment polarity lists that are particular to the community and idealogy associated with each blog. It should be noted that while this method provides better estimates of comment sentiment polarity (as seen in Section 4), it involves more manual work in constructing a seed set than the SentiWordNet method which does not require any manual effort.

3.3 Human labels

As a third method that is accurate but expensive, we manually labeled comments from approximately 30 blog posts from each blog, with a positive or negative label. The guideline in labeling was to determine if the sentiment in the comment section was positive or negative to the subject of the post. The chief intention of this exercise is to determine the quality of the polarity assessments of the SentiWordNet and PMI methods. While it is possible to directly use the assessments and train a classifier, the performance of the classifier will be limited by the very small number of training examples (30 instead of thousands of examples). The accuracy of the two automatic methods to determine comment polarity is shown in Table 2

Blog	SentiWordNet accuracy	PMI accuracy
CB	0.56	0.78
DK	0.54	0.72
MY	0.61	0.83
RS	0.54	0.74
RWN	0.64	0.84

Table 2: Measuring accuracy of automatic comment polarity detection

The better accuracy of the PMI method can be explained by the fact that SentiWordNet is a general purpose list that is not customized for the domain which tends to make it noisy for text in the political domain. The PMI technique corresponds more closely with the human labels but it requires a little human effort in building the initial seed list of positive and negative words.

4 Predicting sentiment from blog content

We now address the problem of using machine learning techniques to predict the polarity of the comments based on the blog post contents.

4.1 SVM

Firstly, we use *support vector machines* (SVM) to perform classification. We frame the classification task as follows: The input features to the classifier are the words in the blog post i.e each blog post is treated as a bag of words and the output variable is the binary comment polarity computed in the previ-

Blog	SentiWordNet		PMI	
	SVM	sLDA	SVM	sLDA
cb	0.56	0.58	0.79	0.79
dk	0.61	0.64	0.75	0.77
my	0.67	0.59	0.87	0.87
rs	0.53	0.55	0.74	0.76
rwn	0.57	0.59	0.90	0.90

Table 3: Accuracy: Using blog posts to predict comment sentiment polarity

ous section. For our experiments, we used the SVM-Light package [6] with a simple linear kernel and evaluated the classifier using 10 fold cross validation.

Table 3 shows the accuracy of the classifier for the different blogs and polarity measuring schemes. The errors in classification can be attributed in part to the inherent difficulty of the task due to the noise of the polarity labeling schemes and in part due to the difficulty in obtaining a signal to *predict comment polarity* from the body of the post.

4.2 Supervised LDA

Next, we use Supervised LDA (sLDA) (Blei and McAuliffe, 2008) to do the classification. sLDA is a model that is an extension of Latent Dirichlet Allocation (LDA) (Blei et al., 2003) that models each document as having an output variable in addition to the document contents. The output variable in the classification case is modeled as an output of a logistic regression model that uses the posterior topic distribution of the LDA model as features. In this task, the output variable is +1 or -1 depending on the polarity of the comment section. In the experiments with sLDA, we set the number of topics as 15 after experimenting with a range of topics and use 10-fold cross validation. The number of topics is set lower than it usually is with topic modeling, due to the relatively short length and small number of documents.

The advantage of sLDA in this task is that we induce topics from the bodies of the blog posts that serve to characterize the different issues that each blog addresses. In addition, the logistic regression parameters indicate how each topic influences the output variable. Table 4 shows the top 1 or 2 topics with the highest negative and positive logistic regression coefficients for each blog. Inspecting the top words of the topics confirms our notions of the kinds of issues that appeal to the readers of each of the blogs. For instance, in the topics induced from Daily Kos, a very liberal leaning blog, we see that the most negative topic (i.e. the topic that contributes the most to potential negative comments) talks about the Bush adminstration and Vice President Cheney, which was and remains quite unpopular with people from the left. The other negative topic concerns the war in Iraq which was also very unpopular within people whose beliefs are liberal-leaning. The most positive topic seemingly focuses on campaign funding. Our conjecture for the high comment polarity is the great success in the then Democratic candidate Obama's fund raising attempts during the presidential campaign. In the second blog, Right Wing News, which is a conservative blog, we see a different picture. The most negative topic deals with Islam and Muslim people which are issues that have tended to evoke negative reactions from certain sections of people with conservative political beliefs. Global warming also evoked negative comments which is consistent with the conservative viewpoint that there isn't evidence to suggest that greenhouse gases cause global warming. The most positive topic seems to be about anti-abortion issues which is an issue that frequently pops up in conservative political discourse. Topics from the other blogs also seem to be in line with the standard positions taken by liberal and conservatives on leading issues in US politics like taxation, immigration, public health and the presidential campaign which was in full flow at the time the data was collected.

Table 3 shows the accuracy of sLDA in predicting the comment polarity based on the blog posts. It can be seen from the table that sLDA performs marginally better than SVM when trained on blog posts, even though documents are now represented in the lower dimensional topic space in contrast to the high dimensional word space that was used with SVM. sLDA provides the additional advantage of providing an overall summary of the corpus via the topic tables it induces.

[6] http://svmlight.joachims.org/

Blog	Topic words	Topic co-efficient
CB	* bush president news administration house white officials report fox government office military department public cheney john journal week pentagon national	-0.79
	* huckabee giuliani romney mccain republican presidential religious campaign gop john party candidate mitt rudy mike conservative thompson support paul candidates	0.48
DK	* bush administration congress law government court house intelligence white executive committee time cheney federal course national act president congressional information	-1.54
	* iraq war bush troops news military american president iraqi starts maine cheers days jeers mccain moreville rightnow day americans people	-0.60
	* money health campaign foster energy district million people nrcc dccc care election time bill change funds don global federal economy	0.62
MY	* iraq war american military iraqi government people troops bush security united forces world country surge presence political force maliki afghanistan	-0.50
	* people care health don public immigration college political education school issue insurance social system policy real lot isn actually sense	1.05
RS	* economy market people financial economic markets money world rate rates federal mortgage government credit prices price term inflation reserve oil	-0.30
	* tax government taxes money economic care people spending million jobs american energy health increase pay economy private free federal business	0.61
RWN	* people muslim world country war american law muslims time police america rights free peace death city islamic government freedom united	-0.68
	* democrats warming global vote election obama energy democratic change votes climate people john gore political gas don voters party bill	-0.39
	* people life women woman time own little love person children world live read believe god isn school feel mean	0.47

Table 4: Topics from sLDA and weights

	SentiWordNet		PMI	
Blog	SVM	sLDA	SVM	sLDA
cb	0.66	0.56	0.79	0.79
dk	0.72	0.59	0.74	0.73
my	0.64	0.61	0.87	0.89
rs	0.65	0.57	0.75	0.80
rwn	0.65	0.60	0.90	0.90

Table 5: Accuracy: Using comments to predict comment sentiment polarity

4.3 Using comments to predict comment polarity

In the previous experiments we were using the bodies of the blog posts to predict comment polarity. There are multiple factors which make this a difficult task. One major factor is the difficulty of learning potentially noisy labels using automatic methods. More interestingly, we operate under the hypothesis that there is signal about comment polarity in the bodies of the blog posts. To test this hypothesis, we train classifiers on the comment sections themselves to predict comment polarity. This serves to eliminate the effect of our hypothesis and focus on the inherent difficulty in learning the noisy labels. Table 5 shows the results of these experiments. We see that once again, sLDA results are comparable to the accuracies reported by SVM and that PMI labels are less noisier than the labels obtained using

Evaluating	Trained on DK	Trained on RWN
DK	0.75/0.77	0.61/0.62
RWN	0.74/0.71	0.90/0.90

Table 6: Cross blog results: Accuracy using SVM/sLDA

SentiWordNet. More importantly, we note that the accuracy in predicting the comment polarity while higher than the accuracy in predicting the polarity from blog posts, is not significantly higher which strongly suggests that blog posts have quite a bit of information regarding comment polarity.

4.4 Cross blog experiments

The effect of the nature of the blog on the classifier is examined by training models on the blog posts from a conservative blog (RWN) using PMI-determined polarities as targets and by testing the model by running liberal blog data (from DK) through it. Similarly, we test RWN blog entries by training it on a classifier trained on DK posts. The results of the experiments are in Table 6. For easy reference, the table also includes the accuracies when blogs are trained using posts from the same blog (obtained from Table 3). We see that the accuracy in predicting polarity degrades when blog posts are tested on a classifier trained on posts from a blog of opposite political affiliation. These results indicate that emotion is tied to the blog and community that one is involved in.

4.5 Conclusion

We addressed the task of predicting the emotional response that is induced in political discourses. To this end, we tackled the tasks of determining the sentiment polarity of comments in blogs and the task of predicting the polarity based on the content of the blog post. Our approach also characterized the issues talked about in specific blog communities. Our experiments show that the community specific PMI method provides a more accurate picture of the sentiment in comments than the generic SentiWordNet technique. We also see that the context of the community is key as seen in the poor performance of models trained on blogs from one end of the political spectrum in predicting the polarity of responses to blog posts in communities on the other end of the spectrum.

References

Andrea Esuli Stefano Baccianella and Fabrizio Sebastiani. 2010. Sentiwordnet 3.0: An enhanced lexical resource for sentiment analysis and opinion mining. In *Proceedings of the Seventh conference on International Language Resources and Evaluation (LREC'10)*, Valletta, Malta, May. European Language Resources Association (ELRA).

David Blei and Jon McAuliffe, 2008. *Supervised Topic Models*, pages 121–128. MIT Press, Cambridge, MA.

D. M Blei, A. Y Ng, and M. I Jordan. 2003. Latent dirichlet allocation. *The Journal of Machine Learning Research*, 3:993–1022.

Li-Ning Huang and Vincent Price. 2001. Motivations, goals, information search, and memory about political candidates. *Political Psychology*, 22(4):pp. 665–692.

Linda M. Isbell, Victor C. Ottati, and Kathleen C. Bruns. 2006. Affect and politics: Effects on judgment, processing, and information seeking. In David Redlawsk, editor, *Feeling Politics: Emotion in Political Information Processing*. Palgrave Macmillan, New York, USA.

Sung-youn Kim, Charles S. Taber, and Milton Lodge. 2008. A Computational Model of the Citizen as Motivated Reasoner: Modeling the Dynamics of the 2000 Presidential Election. *SSRN eLibrary*.

Milton Lodge and Charles Taber, 2000. *Three Steps toward a Theory of Motivated Political Reasoning*. Cambridge University Press.

Brendan O'Connor, Ramnath Balasubramanyan, Bryan R. Routledge, and Noah A. Smith. 2010. From tweets to polls: Linking text sentiment to public opinion time series. In *Proceedings of the International AAAI Conference on Weblogs and Social Media*.

David P. Redlawsk. 2002. Hot cognition or cool consideration? testing the effects of motivated reasoning on political decision making. *The Journal of Politics*, 64(04):1021–1044.

David Redlawsk. 2006. Motivated reasoning, affect, and the role of memory in voter decision-making. In David Redlawsk, editor, *Feeling Politics: Emotion in Political Information Processing*. Palgrave Macmillan, New York, USA.

Andranik Tumasjan, Timm O. Sprenger, Philipp G. Sandner, and Isabell M. Welpe. 2010. Predicting elections with twitter: What 140 characters reveal about political sentiment. In William W. Cohen and Samuel Gosling, editors, *ICWSM*. The AAAI Press.

Peter D. Turney. 2002. Thumbs up or thumbs down?: semantic orientation applied to unsupervised classification of reviews. In *Proceedings of the 40th Annual Meeting on Association for Computational Linguistics*, ACL '02, pages 417–424, Stroudsburg, PA, USA. Association for Computational Linguistics.

Tae. Yano, William. Cohen, and Noah A. Smith. 2009. Predicting response to political blog posts with topic models. In *Proceedings of the North American Association for Computational Linguistics Human Language Technologies Conference*.

Appendix A

Positive	wonderfulness, admirableness, admirability, wonderful, admirable, top-flight, splendid, first-class, fantabulous, excellent, good, balmy, mild, ennoble, dignified, amuse, agree, do_good, benefit, vest, prefer, placate, pacify, mollify, lenify, gentle, conciliate, assuage, appease, filigree, dazzle, admiringly, character, preeminence, note, eminence, distinction, radiance, amiability, bonheur, worship, adoration, divination, music, euphony, judiciousness, essentialness, essentiality, gain, crispness, urbanity, courtesy, decency, modesty, dedication, integrity, honourableness, honorableness, honor, goodness, good, morality, urbanity, tastefulness, elegance, elegance, healthfulness, nutritiveness, nutritiousness, wholesomeness, fineness, choiceness, loveliness, fairness, comeliness, beauteousness, picturesqueness, bluffness, good_nature, character, props, joke, jocularity, jest, worthy, salubrious, healthy, virtuous, esthetic, artistic, aesthetic, spiffing, superlative, sterling, greatest, superb, brilliant, boss, banner, olympian, majestic, straightarrow, wide-eyed, round-eyed, dewy-eyed, childlike, righteous, answerable, nice, decent, diffident, respected, reputable, self-respecting, self-respectful, dignified, constructive, sweet, fabulous, fab, charming, admirable, idyllic, idealized, idealised, ennobling, dignifying, nice, incumbent, clean, lucky, intellectual, formidable, awing, awful, awesome, awe-inspiring, amazing, important, joking, jocular, jocose, jesting, amicable, kind, genial, therapeutic, sanative, remedial, healing, curative, gracious, gainly, goody-goody, good, superb, solid, good, inspired, elysian, divine, worthy, quaint, discerning, golden, fortunate, blest, blessed, courteous, thorough, exhaustive, better, benign, pretty, piquant, engaging, attractive, well, veracious, right, grace, goodwill, belong, accommodate, serve, merit, deserve, shine, radiate, glow, beam, disillusion, disenchant, proclaim, laud, glorify, extol, exalt, cheer, consider, purify, enervate, recuperate, amusingly, dearly, dear, affectionately, thoroughly, soundly, well, simply, time, posterboard, fettle, mildness, clemency, successfulness, prosperity, wellbeing, well-being, upbeat, wholeness, haleness, purity, pureness, innocence, antithesis, serendipity, superordinate, superior, possible, pleaser, idolizer, idoliser, amoralist
Negative	tawdry, shoddy, cheapjack, scrimy, unsound, unfit, bad, sorry, sad, pitiful, lamentable, distressing, deplorable, abject, unfortunate, inauspicious, humbug, trouble, inconvenience, disoblige, bother, smell, stink, reek, twinge, sting, prick, burn, sting, burn, bite, desensitize, desensitise, resent, begrudge, pity, compassionate, abreact, agonize, agonise, muddy, settle, moan, groan, impugn, repudiate, deny, reject, disapprove, snub, repel, rebuff, sting, stick, disapprove, refute, rebut, controvert, foul, curdle, smite, afflict, ease, comfort, ail, inflame, woefully, sadly, lamentably, deplorably, hard, unluckily, unfortunately, regrettably, alas, worst, throe, woe, suffering, inconvenience, incommodiousness, solacement, solace, dyspnoea, dyspnea, throe, shrew, ruffian, rowdy, roughneck, hooligan, bully, plonk, sullenness, moroseness, glumness, moodiness, malignity, malevolence, guilt, sorrow, ruefulness, rue, regret, dolour, dolor, dolefulness, gloating, gloat, weakness, self-torture, self-torment, suffering, hurt, distress, torment, curse, straits, pass, head, excoriation, canard, scurrility, billingsgate, scribble, scrawl, scratch, prejudice, preconception, bias, pill, onus, load, incumbrance, encumbrance, burden, poignancy, pathos, penalty, badness, bad, fault, demerit, hardness, moldiness, harshness, cruelty, cruelness, spitefulness, spite, nastiness, cattiness, bitchiness, malice, malevolency, malevolence, heinousness, barbarousness, barbarity, atrocity, atrociousness, illegitimacy, unnaturalness, disagreeableness, incongruousness, incongruity, ruggedness, hardness, unneighborliness, unfriendliness, disagreeableness, sadness, lugubriousness, gloominess, shlock, schlock, dreck, mongrel, bastard, shenanigan, roguishness, roguery, rascality, mischievousness, mischief-making, mischief, deviltry, devilry, devilment, shitwork, overexertion, overacting, hamming, shlep, schlep, worst, upset, scrofulous, sick, ill, sheltered, occult, trashy, rubbishy, undivided, worried, upset, disturbed, distressed, disquieted, troubled, unmanageable, uncontrollable, mussy, messy, unsympathetic, invalidating, disconfirming, wretched, woeful, miserable, execrable, deplorable, bush-league, bush, tinny, sleazy, punk, crummy, chintzy, cheesy, cheap, bum, inferior, indifferent, lowly, humble, insufficient, deficient, insubordinate, cross-grained, contrarious, spastic, spasmodic, convulsive, unaccepted, unacceptable, nonstandard, unsound, asocial, antisocial, feigned, broken-down, vicious, reprehensible, deplorable, criminal, condemnable, notorious, infamous, ill-famed, untreated, modified, limited, unmixed, unmingled, sheer, plain, cretinous, negative, imponderable, vexing, maddening, infuriating, exasperating, ungrateful, sore, painful, afflictive, harsh, unpeaceable, unforbearing, unpainted, underivative, scurrilous, opprobrious, abusive, verminous, outrageous, horrific, horrid, hideous, creepy, pestilent, pernicious, deadly, baneful, paranormal, grotty, nasty, awful, transcendental, preternatural, otherworldly, nonnatural, simulated, imitation, faux, false, fake, substitute, ersatz, strong, smart, wicked, terrible, severe, unpitying, ruthless, remorseless, pitiless, unlikeable, unlikable, unmourned, unlamented, rough, harsh, woeful, woebegone, lugubrious, heartsick, heartbroken, brokenhearted, bitter

Table 7: Seed words used in the PMI technique

Contextual Bearing on Linguistic Variation in Social Media

Stephan Gouws*, **Donald Metzler**, **Congxing Cai** and **Eduard Hovy**
{gouws, metzler, ccai, hovy}@isi.edu
USC Information Sciences Institute
Marina del Rey, CA
90292, USA

Abstract

Microtexts, like SMS messages, Twitter posts, and Facebook status updates, are a popular medium for real-time communication. In this paper, we investigate the writing conventions that different groups of users use to express themselves in microtexts. Our empirical study investigates properties of lexical transformations as observed within Twitter microtexts. The study reveals that different populations of users exhibit different amounts of shortened English terms and different shortening styles. The results reveal valuable insights into how human language technologies can be effectively applied to microtexts.

1 Introduction

Microtexts, like SMS messages, Twitter posts, and Facebook status updates, are becoming a popular medium for real-time communication in the modern digital age. The ubiquitous nature of mobile phones, tablets, and other Internet-enabled consumer devices provide users with the ability to express what is on their mind nearly anywhere and at just about any time. Since such texts have the potential to provide unique perspectives on human experiences, they have recently become the focus of many studies within the natural language processing and information retrieval research communities.

The informal nature of microtexts allows users to invent *ad hoc* writing conventions that suit their particular needs. These needs strongly depend on various user contexts, such as their age, geographic location, how they want to be outwardly perceived, and so on. Hence, social factors influence the way that users express themselves in microtexts and other forms of media.

In addition to social influences, there are also usability and interface issues that may affect the way a user communicates using microtexts. For example, the Twitter microblog service imposes an explicit message length limit of 140 characters. Users of such services also often send messages using mobile devices. There may be high input costs associated with using mobile phone keypads, thus directly impacting the nature of how users express themselves.

In this paper, we look specifically at understanding the writing conventions that different groups of users use to express themselves. This is accomplished by carrying out a novel empirical investigation of the lexical transformation characteristics observed within Twitter microtexts. Our empirical evaluation includes: (i) an analysis of how frequently different user populations apply lexical transformations, and (ii) a study of the types of transformations commonly employed by different populations of users. We investigate several ways of defining user populations (e.g., based on the Twitter client, time zone, etc.). Our results suggest that not all microtexts are created equal, and that certain populations of users are much more likely to use certain types of lexical transformations than others.

This paper has two primary contributions. First, we present a novel methodology for contextualized analysis of lexical transformations found within mi-

*This work was done while the first author was a visiting student at ISI from the MIH Media Lab at Stellenbosch University, South Africa. Correspondence may alternatively be directed to stephan@ml.sun.ac.za.

crotexts. The methodology leverages recent advances in automated techniques for cleaning noisy text. This approach enables us to study the frequency and types of transformations that are common within different user populations and user contexts. Second, we present results from an empirical evaluation over microtexts collected from the Twitter microblog service. Our empirical analysis reveals that within Twitter microtexts, different user populations and user contexts give rise to different forms of expression, by way of different styles of lexical transformations.

The remainder of this paper is laid out as follows. Section 2 describes related work, while Section 3 motivates our investigation. Our multi-pronged methodology for analyzing lexical transformations is described in Section 4. Section 5 describes our experimental results. Finally, Section 6 concludes the paper and describes possible directions for future work.

2 Related Work

Although our work is primarily focused on analyzing the lexical variation in language found in online social media, our analysis methodology makes strong use of techniques for normalizing 'noisy text' such as SMS-messages and Twitter messages into standard English.

Normalizing text can traditionally be approached using three well-known NLP metaphors, namely that of spell-checking, machine translation (MT) and automatic speech recognition (ASR) (Kobus et al., 2008).

In the spell-checking approach, corrections from 'noisy' words to 'clean' words proceed on a word-by-word basis. Choudhury (2007) implements the noisy channel model (Shannon and Weaver, 1948) using a hidden Markov model to handle both graphemic and phonemic variations, and Cook and Stevenson (2009) improve on this model by adapting the channel noise according to several predefined word formations such as stylistic variation, word clipping, etc. However, spelling correction is traditionally conducted in media with relatively high percentages of well-formed text where one can perform word boundary detection and thus tokenization to a high degree of accuracy. The main drawback is the strong confidence this approach places on word boundaries (Beaufort et al., 2010), since detecting word boundaries in noisy text is not a trivial problem.

In the machine translation approach (Bangalore et al., 2002; Aw et al., 2006), normalizing noisy text is considered as a translation task from a source language (the noisy text) to a target language (the cleansed text). Since noisy- and clean text typically vary wildly, it satisfies the notion of translating between two languages. However, since these transformations can be highly creative, they usually need a wide context (more than one word) to be resolved adequately. Kobus (2008) also points out that despite the fairly good results achieved with this system, such a purely phrase-based translation model cannot adequately handle the wide level of lexical creativity found in these media.

Finally, the ASR approach is based on the observation that many noisy word forms in SMSes or other noisy text are based on phonetic plays of the clean word. This approach starts by converting the input message into a phone lattice, which is converted to a word lattice using a phoneme-grapheme dictionary. Finally the word lattice is decoded by applying a language model to the word lattice and using a best-path algorithm to recover the most likely original word sequence. This approach has the advantage of being able to handle badly segmented word boundaries efficiently, however it prevents the next normalization steps from knowing what graphemes were in the initial sequence (Kobus et al., 2008).

What fundamentally separates the noisy text cleansing task from the spell-checking problem is that most often lexical ill-formedness in these media is *intentional*. Han (2011) proposes that this might be in an attempt to save characters in length-constrained media (such as Twitter or SMS), for social identity (conversing in the dialect of a specific group), or due to convention of the medium. Emotional context is typically expressed with repeat characters such as 'I am sooooooo tired' or excessive punctuation. At times, however, out-of-vocabulary tokens (spelling errors) might result purely as the result of cognitive oversight.

Cook and Stevenson (2009) are one of the first to explicitly analyze the *types* of transformations found in short message domains. They identify: 1) stylistic variation (better→betta), 2) subsequence abbreviation (doing→dng), 3) clipping of the letter 'g' (talking→talkin), 4) clipping of 'h' (hello→ello), and 5) general syllable clipping (anyway→neway), to be the most frequent transformations. Cook and Stevenson then incorporate these transformations into their model. The idea is that such an unsupervised approach based on the linguistic properties of creative word forms has the potential to be adapted for normalization in other similar genres without the cost of developing a large training corpus. Most importantly, they find that many creative texting forms are the result of a *small* number of specific word formation processes.

Han (2011) performs a simple analysis on the out-of-vocabulary words found in Twitter, and find that the majority of ill-formed words in Twitter can be attributed to instances where letters are missing or where there are extraneous letters, but the lexical correspondence to the target word is trivially accessible. They find that most ill-formed words are based on morphophonemic variations.

3 Motivation

All of the previous work described in Section 2 either

i) only focus on recovering the most likely 'standard English' form of a message, disregarding the stylistic structure of the original noisy text, or

ii) considers the structure of the noisy text found in a medium as a whole, only as a first step (the means) to identify common types of noisy transformations which can subsequently be accounted for (or 'corrected') to produce normalized messages (the desired end result).

However, based on the fact that language is highly contextual, we ask the question: What influence does the *context* in which a message is produced have on the resulting observed surface structure and style of the message?

In general, since some topics are for instance more formal or informal than others, vocabulary and linguistic style often changes based on the topic that is being discussed. Moreover, in social media one can identify several other types of context. Specifically in Twitter, one might consider a user's geographical location, the client from which a user is broadcasting her message, how long she has been using the Twitter service, and so forth.

The intuition is that the unconstrained nature of these media afford users the ability to invent writing conventions to suit their needs. Since users' needs depend on their circumstances, and hence their context, we hypothesize that the observed writing systems might be influenced by some elements of their context. For instance, phonemic writing systems might be related to a user's dialect which is related to a user's geographical location. Furthermore, highly compressed writing conventions (throwing away vowels, using prefixes of words, etc.) might result from the relatively high input cost associated with using unwieldy keypads on some mobile clients, etc.

The present work is focused on looking at these stylistic elements of messages found in social media, by analyzing the types of stylistic variation at the lexical level, across these contextual dimensions.

4 Method

In the following discussion we make a distinction between *within-tweet context* and the general *message-context* in which a message is created. Within-tweet context is the linguistic context (the other terms) that envelopes a term in a Twitter message. The general context of a Twitter message is the observable elements of the environment in which it was conceived. For the current study, we record

1. the user's **location**, and

2. the **client** from which the message was sent,

We follow a two-pronged analytic approach: Firstly, we conduct a naïve, context-free analysis (at the linguistic level) of all words not commonly found in standard, everyday English. This analysis purely looks at the terminology that are found on Twitter, and does not attempt to normalize these messages in any way. Therefore, different surface forms of the same word, such as 'today', '2day', '2d4y', are all considered distinct terms. We then analyse the terminology over different contextual dimensions such as client and location.

Secondly, we perform a more in-depth and *contextual* analysis (at the word level) by first normalizing the potentially noisy message to recover the most likely surface form of the message and recording the types of changes that were made, and then analyzing these types of changes across different general contextual dimensions (client and location).

As noted in Section 2, text message normalization is not a trivial process. As shown by Han (2011), most transformations from in-vocabulary words to out-of-vocabulary words can be attributed to a single letter that is changed, removed, or added. Furthermore, they note that most ill-formed words are related to some morphophonemic variation. We therefore implemented a text cleanser based on the design of Contractor (2010) using pre-processing techniques discussed in (Kaufmann and Kalita, 2010).

It works as follows: For each input message, we replace @-usernames with "*USR*" and urls with "*URL*". Hash tags can either be part of the sentence ('just got a #droid today') or be peripheral to the sentence ('what a loooong day! #wasted'). Following Kaufmann (2010) we remove hashtags at the end of messages when they are preceded by typical end-of-sentence punctuation marks. Hash tags in the middle of messages are retained, and the hash sign removed.

Next we tokenize this preprocessed message using the NLTK tokenizer (Loper and Bird, 2002). As noted earlier, standard NLP tools do not perform well on noisy text out-of-the-box. Based on inspection of incorrectly tokenized output, we therefore include a post-tokenization phase where we split all tokens that include a punctuation symbol into the individual one or two alphanumeric tokens (on either side of the punctuation symbol), and the punctuation symbol[1]. This heuristic catches most cases of run-on sentences.

Given a set of input tokens, we process these one by one, by comparing each token to the words in the lexicon L and constructing a confusion network CN. Each in-vocabulary term, punctuation token or other valid-but-not-in-vocabulary term is added to CN with probability 1.0 as shown in Algorithm 1.

Character	Transliteration candidates
1	'1', 'l', 'one'
2	'2', 'to', 'too', 'two'
3	'3', 'e', 'three'
4	'4', 'a', 'for', 'four'
5	'5', 's', 'five'
6	'6', 'b', 'six'
7	'7', 't', 'seven'
8	'8', 'ate', 'eight'
9	'9', 'g', 'nine'
0	'0', 'o', 'zero'
'@'	'@', 'at'
'&'	'&', 'and'

Table 1: Transliteration lookup table.

valid_tok(w_i) checks for "*USR*", "*URL*", or any token longer than 1 character with no alphabetical characters. This heuristic retains tokens such as '9-11', '12:44', etc.

At this stage, all out-of-vocabulary (OOV) terms represent the terms that we are uncertain about, and hence candidate terms for cleansing. First, for each OOV term, we enumerate each possibly ambiguous character into all its possible interpretations with the transliteration table shown in Table 1. This expands, for example, 't0day' → ['t0day', 'today'], and also '2day' → ['2day', 'twoday', 'today'], etc.

Each transliterated candidate word in each confusion set produced this way is then scored with the original word and ranked using the heuristic function (`sim()`) described in (Contractor et al., 2010)[2]. We also evaluated a purely phonetic edit-distance similarity function, based on the Double Metaphone algorithm (Philips, 2000), but found the string-similarity-based function to give more reliable results.

Each confusion set produced this way (see Algorithm 2) is joined to its previous set to form a growing confusion lattice. Finally this lattice is decoded by converting it into the probabilistic finite-state grammar format, and by using the SRI-LM toolkit's (Stolcke, 2002) `lattice-tool` command to find the best path through the lattice by

[1]This is easily accomplished using a regular expression group-substitution of the form `(\w*)([P])(\w*)`→`[\1, \2, \3]`, where `\w` represents the set of alphanumeric characters, and `P` is the set of all punctuation marks `[.,;'"...]`

[2]The longest common subsequence between the two words, normalized by the edit distances between their consonant skeletons.

Transformation Type	Rel %
single_char ("see" → "c")	29.1%
suffix ("why" → "y")	18.8%
drop_vowels ("be" → "b")	16.4%
prefix ("tomorrow" → "tom")	9.0%
you_to_u ("you" → "u")	8.3%
drop_last_char ("running" → "runnin")	7.0%
repeat_letter ("so" → "soooo")	5.5%
contraction ("you will" → "you'll")	5.0%
th_to_d ("this" → "dis")	1.0%

Table 2: Most frequently observed types of transformations with an example in parentheses. *Rel %* shows the relative percentage of the top-10 transformations which were identified (excluding unidentified transformations) to belong to a specific class.

making use of a language model to promote fluidity in the text, and trained as follows:

We generated a corpus containing roughly 10M tokens of clean English tweets. We used a simple heuristic for selecting clean tweets: For each tweet we computed if $\frac{\#(OOV)}{\#(IV)+1} < \rho$, where $\rho = 0.5$ was found to give good results. On this corpus we trained a trigram language model, using Good-Turing smoothing. Next, a subset of the LA Times containing 30M words was used to train a 'general English' language model in the same way. These two models were combined[3] in the ratio 0.7 to 0.3.

The result of the decoding process is the hypothesized clean tokens of the original sentence. Whenever the cleanser makes a substitution, it is recorded for further analysis. Upon closer inspection, it was found that most transformation types can be recognized by using a fairly simple post-processing step. Table 2 lists the most frequent types of transformations. While these transformations do not have perfect coverage, they account for over 90% of the (correct) transformations produced by the cleanser. The rules fail to cover relatively infrequent edge cases, such as "l8r → later", "cuz → because", "dha → the", and "yep → yes" [4].

Original	Cleansed
Swet baby jeebus, someone PLEASE WINE ME!	sweet baby jesus , someone please wine me !
2 years with Katie today!	two years with katie today!
k,hope nobody was hurt.gud mornin jare	okay , hope nobody was hurt . good morning jamie
When u a bum but think u da best person on da court you doodooforthebooboo	when you a bum but think you the best person on the court you dorothy
NYC premiere 2morrow.	nice premiere tomorrow .

Table 3: Examples of original and automatically cleansed versions of Twitter messages.

Algorithm 1 Main cleanser algorithm pseudo code. The `decode()` command converts the confusion network (CN) into PFSG format and decodes it using the `lattice-tool` of the SRI-LM toolkit.

Require: Lexicon L, Punctuation set P
  function CLEANSE_MAIN(M_{in})
    for $w_i \in M_{\text{in}}$ **do**
      if $w_i \in L \cup P$ or valid_tok(w_i) **then**
        Add $(1.0, w_i)$ to CN_{out} ▷ Probability 1.0
      else
        Add conf_set(w_i) to CN_{out}
      end if
    end for
    return decode(CN_{out})
  end function

Table 3 illustrates some example corrections made by the cleanser. As the results show, the cleanser is able to correct many of the more common types of transformations, but can fail when it encounters infrequent or out-of-vocabulary terms.

5 Evaluation

This section describes our empirical evaluation and analysis of how users in different contexts express themselves differently using microtexts. We focus specifically on the types of lexical transformations that are commonly applied globally, within populations of users, and in a contextualized manner.

[3]Using the `-mix-lm` and `-lambda` and `-mix-lambda2` options to the SRI-LM toolkit's `ngram` module.

[4]To our surprise these 'typical texting forms' disappeared into the long tail in our data set.

Algorithm 2 Algorithm pseudo code for generating confusion set CS. $L[w_i]$ is the lexicon partitioning function for word w_i.

Require: Lexicon L, confusion set CS, implemented as top-K heap containing (s_i, w_i), indexed on s_i

```
function CONF_SET(w_i)
    W ← translits(w_i)
    for w_j ∈ W do
        for w_k ∈ L[w_j] do
            s_k ← sim(w_j, w_k)
            if s_k > min(CS) then
                Add (s_k, w_k) to CS
            end if
        end for
    end for
    return CS
end function
```

5.1 Out-of-Vocabulary Analysis

We begin by analyzing the types of terms that are common in microtexts but not typically used in proper, everyday English texts (such as newspapers). We refer to such terms as being *out-of-vocabulary*, since they are not part of the common written English lexicon. The goal of this analysis is to understand how different contexts affect the number of out-of-vocabulary terms found in microtexts. We hypothesize that certain contextual factors may influence a user's ability (or interest) to formulate clean microtexts that only contain common English terms.

We ran our analysis over a collection of one million Twitter messages collected using the Twitter streaming API during 2010. Tweets gathered from the Twitter API are tagged with a language identifier that indicates the language a user has chosen for his or her account. However, we found that many tweets purported to be English were in fact not. Hence, we ran all of the tweets gathered through a simple English language classifier that was trained using a small set of manually labeled tweets, uses character trigrams and average word length as features, and achieves an accuracy of around 93%. The everyday written English lexicon, which we treat as the "gold standard" lexicon, was distilled from the same collection of LA Times news articles described in Section 4. This yielded a comprehensive lexicon of approximately half a million terms.

Timezone	% In-Vocabulary
Australia	86%
UK	85%
US (Atlantic)	84%
Hong Kong	83%
US (Pacific)	81%
Hawaii	81%
Overall	81%

Table 4: Percentage of in-vocabulary found in large English lexicon for different geographic locations.

For each tweet, the tokenized terms were looked up in the LA Times lexicon to determine if the term was out-of-vocabulary or not. Not surprisingly, the most frequent out-of-vocabulary terms identified are Twitter usernames, URLs, hasthags, and RT (the terminology for a re-broadcast, or re-tweeted, message). These tokens alone account for approximately half of all out-of-vocabulary tokens. The most frequent out-of-vocabulary terms include "lol", "haha", "gonna", "lmao", "wanna", "omg", "gotta". Numerous expletives also appear amongst the most common out-of-vocabulary terms, since such terms never appear in the LA Times. Out of vocabulary terms make up 19% of all terms in our data set.

In the remainder of this section, we examine the out-of-vocabulary properties of different populations of users based on their geographic location and their client (e.g., Web-based or mobile phone-based).

5.1.1 Geographic Locations

To analyze the out-of-vocabulary properties of users in different geographic locations, we extracted the time zone information from each Tweet in our data set. Although Twitter allows users to specify their location, many users leave this field blank, use informal terminology ("lower east side"), or fabricate non-existent locations (e.g., "wherever i want to be"). Therefore, we use the user's time zone as a proxy for their actual location, in hopes that users have less incentive to provide incorrect information.

For the Twitter messages associated with a given time zone, we computed the percentage of tokens found within our LA Times-based lexicon. The results from this analysis are provided in Table 4. It is

Client	% In-Vocabulary
Facebook	88%
Twitter for iPhone	84%
Twitter for Blackberry	83%
Web	82%
UberTwitter	78%
Snaptu	73%
Overall	81%

Table 5: Percentage of in-vocabulary found in large English lexicon for different Twitter clients.

important to note that these results were computed over hundreds of thousands of tokens, and hence the variance of our estimates is very small. This means that the differences observed here are statistically meaningful, even though the absolute differences tend to be somewhat small.

These results indicate that microtexts composed by users in different geographic locations exhibit different amounts of out-of-vocabulary terms. Users in Australia, the United Kingdom, Hong Kong, and the East Coast of the United States (e.g., New York City) include fewer out-of-vocabulary terms in their Tweets than average. However, users from the West Coast of the United States (e.g., Los Angeles, CA) and Hawaii are on-par with the overall average, but include 5% more out-of-vocabulary terms than the Australian users.

As expected, the locations with fewer-than-average in-vocabulary tokens are associated with non-English speaking countries, despite the output from the classifier.

5.1.2 Twitter Clients

In a similar experiment, we also investigated the frequency of out-of-vocabulary terms conditioned on the Twitter client (or "source") used to compose the message. Example Twitter clients include the Web-based client at `www.twitter.com`, official Twitter clients for specific mobile platforms (e.g., iPhone, Android, etc.), and third-party clients. Each client has its own characteristics, target user base, and features.

In Table 5, we show the percentage of in-vocabulary terms for a sample of the most widely used Twitter clients. Unlike the geographic location-based analysis, which showed only minor differences amongst the user populations, we see much more dramatic differences here. Some clients, such as Facebook, which provides a way of cross-posting status updates between the two services, has the largest percentage of in-vocabulary terms of the major clients in our data.

One interesting, but unexpected, finding is that the mobile phone (i.e., iPhone and Blackberry) clients have *fewer* out-of-vocabulary terms, on average, than the Web-based client. This suggests that either the users of the clients are less likely to misspell words or use slang terminology or that the clients may have better or more intuitive spell checking capabilities. A more thorough analysis is necessary to better understand the root cause of this phenomenon.

At the other end of the spectrum are the UberTwitter and Snaptu clients, which exhibit a substantially larger number of out-of-vocabulary terms. These clients are also typically used on mobile devices. As with our previous analysis, it is difficult to pinpoint the exact cause of such behavior, but we hypothesize that it is a function of user demographics and difficulties associated with inputting text on mobile devices.

5.2 Contextual Analysis

In this section, we test the hypothesis that different user populations make use of different *types* of lexical transformations. To achieve this goal, we make use of our noisy text cleanser. For each Twitter message run through the cleanser, we record the original and cleaned version of each term. For all of the terms that the cleanser corrects, we automatically identify which (if any) of the transformation rules listed in Table 2 explain the transformation between the original and clean version of the term. We use this output to analyze the distribution of transformations observed across different user populations.

We begin by analyzing the types of transformations observed across Twitter clients. Figure 1 plots the (normalized) distribution of lexical transformations observed for the Web, Twitter for Blackberry, Twitter for iPhone, and UberTwitter clients, grouped by the transformations. We also group the transformations by the individual clients in Figure 2 for more direct comparison.

The results show that Web users tend to use more

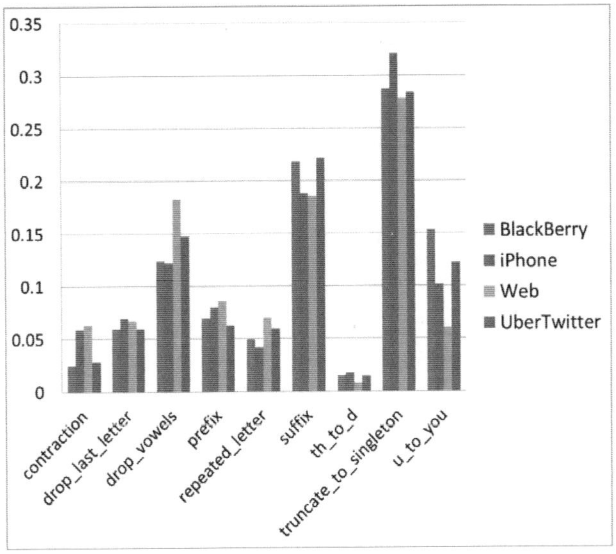

Figure 1: Proportion of transformations observed across Twitter clients, grouped by transformation type.

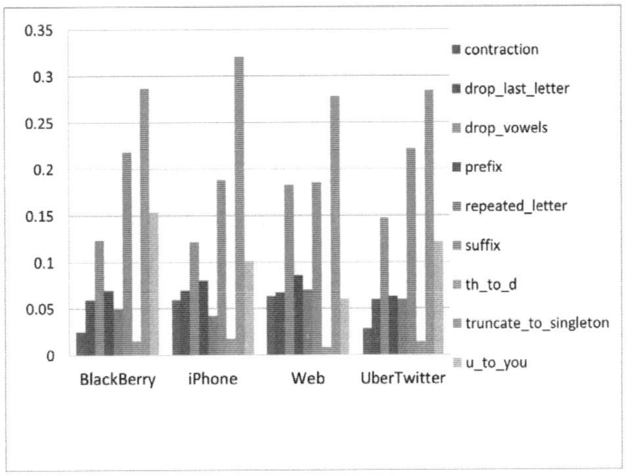

Figure 2: Proportion of transformations observed across Twitter clients, grouped by client.

contractions than Blackberry and UberTwitter users. We relate this result to the differences in typing on a virtual compared to a multi-touch keypad. It was surprising to see that iPhone users tended to use considerably more contractions than the other mobile device clients, which we relate to its word-prediction functionality. Another interesting result is the fact that Web users often drop vowels to shorten terms more than their mobile client counterparts. Instead, mobile users often use suffix-style transformations more, which is often more aggressive than the dropping vowels transformation, and possibly a result of the pervasiveness of mobile phones: Large populations of people's first interaction with technology these days are through a mobile phone, a device where strict length limits are imposed on texting, and which hence enforce habits of aggressive lexical compression, which might transfer directly to their use of PCs. Finally, we observe that mobile device users replace "you" with "u" substantially more than users of the Web client.

We also performed the same analysis across time zones/locations. The results are presented in Figure 3 by transformation-type, and again grouped by location for direct comparison in Figure 4. We observe, perhaps not surprisingly, that the East Coast US, West Coast US, and Hawaii are the most similar with respect to the types of transformations that they commonly use. However, the most interesting finding here is that British users tend to utilize a noticeably different set of transformations than American users in the Pacific time zones. For example, British users are much more likely to use contractions and suffixes, but far less likely to drop the last letter of a word, drop all of the vowels in a word, use prefix-style transformations, or to repeat a given letter multiple times. In a certain sense, this suggests that British users tend to write more proper, less informal English and make use of strikingly different styles for shortening words compared to American users. This might be related to the differences in dialects between the two regions manifesting itself during a process of phonetic transliteration when composing the messages: Inhabitants of the south-west regions in the US are known for pronouncing for instance *running* as *runnin'*, which manifests as dropping the last letter, and so forth.

Therefore, when taken with our out-of-vocabulary analysis, our experimental evaluation shows clear evidence that different populations of users express themselves differently online and use different types of lexical transformations depending on their context. It is our hope that the outcome of this study will spark further investigation into these types of issues and ultimately lead to effective contextually-aware natural language processing and information retrieval approaches that can adapt to a wide range of user contexts.

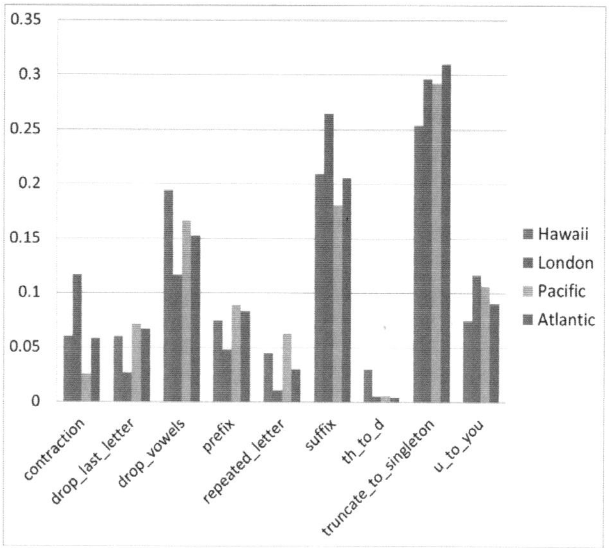

Figure 3: Proportion of transformations observed across geographic locations, grouped by transformation type.

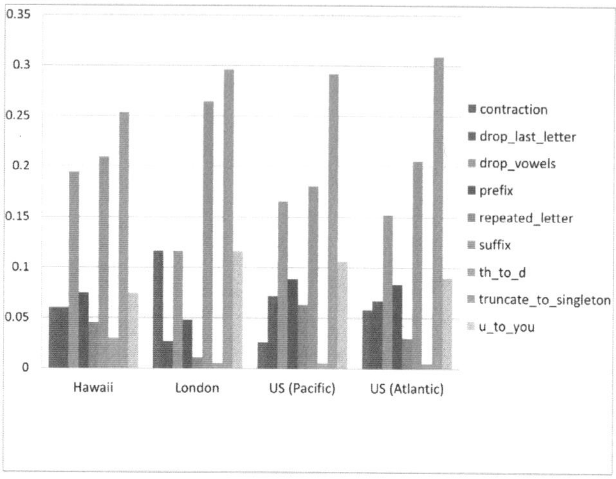

Figure 4: Proportion of transformations observed across geographic locations, grouped by location.

6 Conclusions and Future Work

This paper investigated the writing conventions that different groups of users use to express themselves in microtexts. We analyzed characteristics of terms that are commonly found in English Twitter messages but are never seen within a large collection of LA Times news articles. The results showed that a very small number of terms account for a large proportion of the out-of-vocabulary terms. The same analysis revealed that different populations of users exhibit different propensities to use out-of-vocabulary terms. For example, it was found that British users tend to use fewer out-of-vocabulary terms compared to users within the United States.

We also carried out a contextualized analysis that leveraged a state-of-the-art noisy text cleanser. By analyzing the most common types of lexical transformations, it was observed that the types of transformations used varied across Twitter clients (e.g., Web-based clients vs. mobile phone-based clients) and geographic location. This evidence supported our hypothesis that the measurable contextual indicators surrounding messages in social media play an important role in determining how messages in these media vary at the surface (lexical) level from what might be considered standard English.

The outcome of our empirical evaluation and subsequent analysis suggests that human language technologies (especially natural language processing techniques that rely on well-formed inputs) are likely to be highly susceptible to failure as the result of lexical transformations across nearly all populations and contexts. However, certain simple rules can be used to clean up a large number of out-of-vocabulary tokens. Unfortunately, such rules would not be able to properly correct the long tail of the out-of-vocabulary distribution. In such cases, more sophisticated approaches, such as the noisy text cleanser used in this work, are necessary to combat the noise. Interestingly, most of the lexical transformations observed affect non-content words, which means that most information retrieval techniques will be unaffected by such transformations.

As part of future work, we are generally interested in developing population and/or context-aware language processing and understanding techniques on top of microtexts. We are also interested in analyzing different user contexts, such as those based on age and gender and to empirically quantify the effect of noise on actual natural language processing and information retrieval tasks, such as part of speech tagging, parsing, summarization, etc.

Acknowledgments

We would like to thank the anonymous reviewers for their insightful comments. Stephan Gouws would like to thank MIH Holdings Ltd. for financial support during the course of this work.

References

A.T. Aw, M. Zhang, J. Xiao, and J. Su. 2006. A Phrase-based Statistical Model for SMS Text Normalization. In *Proceedings of the COLING/ACL Main Conference Poster Sessions*, pages 33–40. Association for Computational Linguistics.

S. Bangalore, V. Murdock, and G. Riccardi. 2002. Bootstrapping Bilingual Data Using Consensus Translation for a Multilingual Instant Messaging System. In *Proceedings of the 19th International Conference on Computational Linguistics-Volume 1*, pages 1–7. Association for Computational Linguistics.

R. Beaufort, S. Roekhaut, L.A. Cougnon, and C. Fairon. 2010. A Hybrid Rule/Model-based Finite-State Framework for Normalizing SMS Messages. In *Proceedings of the 48th Annual Meeting of the Association for Computational Linguistics*, pages 770–779. Association for Computational Linguistics.

M. Choudhury, R. Saraf, V. Jain, A. Mukherjee, S. Sarkar, and A. Basu. 2007. Investigation and Modeling of the Structure of Texting Language. *International Journal on Document Analysis and Recognition*, 10(3):157–174.

D. Contractor, T.A. Faruquie, and L.V. Subramaniam. 2010. Unsupervised Cleansing of Noisy Text. In *Proceedings of the 23rd International Conference on Computational Linguistics: Posters*, pages 189–196. Association for Computational Linguistics.

P. Cook and S. Stevenson. 2009. An Unsupervised Model for Text Message Normalization. In *Proceedings of the Workshop on Computational Approaches to Linguistic Creativity*, pages 71–78. Association for Computational Linguistics.

Bo Han and Timothy Baldwin. 2011. Lexical Normalisation of Short Text Messages: Makn Sens a #twitter. In *Proceedings of the 49th Annual Meeting of the Association for Computational Linguistics: Human Language Technologies*. Association for Computational Linguistics.

M. Kaufmann and J. Kalita. 2010. Syntactic Normalization of Twitter Messages.

C. Kobus, F. Yvon, and G. Damnati. 2008. Normalizing SMS: Are Two Metaphors Better Than One? In *Proceedings of the 22nd International Conference on Computational Linguistics-Volume 1*, pages 441–448. Association for Computational Linguistics.

E. Loper and S. Bird. 2002. NLTK: The Natural Language Toolkit. In *Proceedings of the ACL-02 Workshop on Effective tools and Methodologies for Teaching Natural Language Processing and Computational Linguistics-Volume 1*, pages 63–70. Association for Computational Linguistics.

L. Philips. 2000. The Double Metaphone Search Algorithm. *CC Plus Plus Users Journal*, 18(6):38–43.

C.E. Shannon and W. Weaver. 1948. The Mathematical Theory of Communication. *Bell System Technical Journal*, 27:623–656.

A. Stolcke. 2002. SRILM - An Extensible Language Modeling Toolkit. In *Proceedings of the International Conference on Spoken Language Processing*, volume 2, pages 901–904.

Sentiment Analysis of Twitter Data

Apoorv Agarwal Boyi Xie Ilia Vovsha Owen Rambow Rebecca Passonneau
Department of Computer Science
Columbia University
New York, NY 10027 USA
{apoorv@cs, xie@cs, iv2121@, rambow@ccls, becky@cs}.columbia.edu

Abstract

We examine sentiment analysis on Twitter data. The contributions of this paper are: (1) We introduce POS-specific prior polarity features. (2) We explore the use of a tree kernel to obviate the need for tedious feature engineering. The new features (in conjunction with previously proposed features) and the tree kernel perform approximately at the same level, both outperforming the state-of-the-art baseline.

1 Introduction

Microblogging websites have evolved to become a source of varied kind of information. This is due to nature of microblogs on which people post real time messages about their opinions on a variety of topics, discuss current issues, complain, and express positive sentiment for products they use in daily life. In fact, companies manufacturing such products have started to poll these microblogs to get a sense of general sentiment for their product. Many times these companies study user reactions and reply to users on microblogs. One challenge is to build technology to detect and summarize an overall sentiment.

In this paper, we look at one such popular microblog called Twitter and build models for classifying "tweets" into positive, negative and neutral sentiment. We build models for two classification tasks: a binary task of classifying sentiment into positive and negative classes and a 3-way task of classifying sentiment into positive, negative and neutral classes. We experiment with three types of models: unigram model, a feature based model and a tree kernel based model. For the feature based model we use some of the features proposed in past literature and propose new features. For the tree kernel based model we design a new tree representation for tweets. We use a unigram model, previously shown to work well for sentiment analysis for Twitter data, as our baseline. Our experiments show that a unigram model is indeed a hard baseline achieving over 20% over the chance baseline for both classification tasks. Our feature based model that uses only 100 features achieves similar accuracy as the unigram model that uses over 10,000 features. Our tree kernel based model outperforms both these models by a significant margin. We also experiment with a combination of models: combining unigrams with our features and combining our features with the tree kernel. Both these combinations outperform the unigram baseline by over 4% for both classification tasks. In this paper, we present extensive feature analysis of the 100 features we propose. Our experiments show that features that have to do with Twitter-specific features (emoticons, hashtags etc.) add value to the classifier but only marginally. Features that combine prior polarity of words with their parts-of-speech tags are most important for both the classification tasks. Thus, we see that standard natural language processing tools are useful even in a genre which is quite different from the genre on which they were trained (newswire). Furthermore, we also show that the tree kernel model performs roughly as well as the best feature based models, even though it does not require detailed feature engineering.

We use manually annotated Twitter data for our

experiments. One advantage of this data, over previously used data-sets, is that the tweets are collected in a streaming fashion and therefore represent a true sample of actual tweets in terms of language use and content. Our new data set is available to other researchers. In this paper we also introduce two resources which are available (contact the first author): 1) a hand annotated dictionary for emoticons that maps emoticons to their polarity and 2) an acronym dictionary collected from the web with English translations of over 5000 frequently used acronyms.

The rest of the paper is organized as follows. In section 2, we discuss classification tasks like sentiment analysis on micro-blog data. In section 3, we give details about the data. In section 4 we discuss our pre-processing technique and additional resources. In section 5 we present our prior polarity scoring scheme. In section 6 we present the design of our tree kernel. In section 7 we give details of our feature based approach. In section 8 we present our experiments and discuss the results. We conclude and give future directions of research in section 9.

2 Literature Survey

Sentiment analysis has been handled as a Natural Language Processing task at many levels of granularity. Starting from being a document level classification task (Turney, 2002; Pang and Lee, 2004), it has been handled at the sentence level (Hu and Liu, 2004; Kim and Hovy, 2004) and more recently at the phrase level (Wilson et al., 2005; Agarwal et al., 2009).

Microblog data like Twitter, on which users post real time reactions to and opinions about "everything", poses newer and different challenges. Some of the early and recent results on sentiment analysis of Twitter data are by Go et al. (2009), (Bermingham and Smeaton, 2010) and Pak and Paroubek (2010). Go et al. (2009) use distant learning to acquire sentiment data. They use tweets ending in positive emoticons like ":)" ":-)" as positive and negative emoticons like ":(" ":-(" as negative. They build models using Naive Bayes, MaxEnt and Support Vector Machines (SVM), and they report SVM outperforms other classifiers. In terms of feature space, they try a Unigram, Bigram model in conjunction with parts-of-speech (POS) features. They note that the unigram model outperforms all other models. Specifically, bigrams and POS features do not help. Pak and Paroubek (2010) collect data following a similar distant learning paradigm. They perform a different classification task though: subjective versus objective. For subjective data they collect the tweets ending with emoticons in the same manner as Go et al. (2009). For objective data they crawl twitter accounts of popular newspapers like "New York Times", "Washington Posts" etc. They report that POS and bigrams both help (contrary to results presented by Go et al. (2009)). Both these approaches, however, are primarily based on ngram models. Moreover, the data they use for training and testing is collected by search queries and is therefore biased. In contrast, we present features that achieve a significant gain over a unigram baseline. In addition we explore a different method of data representation and report significant improvement over the unigram models. Another contribution of this paper is that we report results on manually annotated data that does not suffer from any known biases. Our data is a random sample of streaming tweets unlike data collected by using specific queries. The size of our hand-labeled data allows us to perform cross-validation experiments and check for the variance in performance of the classifier across folds.

Another significant effort for sentiment classification on Twitter data is by Barbosa and Feng (2010). They use polarity predictions from three websites as noisy labels to train a model and use 1000 manually labeled tweets for tuning and another 1000 manually labeled tweets for testing. They however do not mention how they collect their test data. They propose the use of syntax features of tweets like retweet, hashtags, link, punctuation and exclamation marks in conjunction with features like prior polarity of words and POS of words. We extend their approach by using real valued prior polarity, and by combining prior polarity with POS. Our results show that the features that enhance the performance of our classifiers the most are features that combine prior polarity of words with their parts of speech. The tweet syntax features help but only marginally.

Gamon (2004) perform sentiment analysis on feeadback data from Global Support Services survey. One aim of their paper is to analyze the role of linguistic features like POS tags. They perform extensive feature analysis and feature selection and demonstrate that abstract linguistic analysis features contributes to the classifier accuracy. In this paper we perform extensive feature analysis and show that the use of only 100 abstract linguistic features performs as well as a hard unigram baseline.

3 Data Description

Twitter is a social networking and microblogging service that allows users to post real time messages, called tweets. Tweets are short messages, restricted to 140 characters in length. Due to the nature of this microblogging service (quick and short messages), people use acronyms, make spelling mistakes, use emoticons and other characters that express special meanings. Following is a brief terminology associated with tweets. Emoticons: These are facial expressions pictorially represented using punctuation and letters; they express the user's mood. Target: Users of Twitter use the "@" symbol to refer to other users on the microblog. Referring to other users in this manner automatically alerts them. Hashtags: Users usually use hashtags to mark topics. This is primarily done to increase the visibility of their tweets.

We acquire 11,875 manually annotated Twitter data (tweets) from a commercial source. They have made part of their data publicly available. For information on how to obtain the data, see Acknowledgments section at the end of the paper. They collected the data by archiving the real-time stream. No language, location or any other kind of restriction was made during the streaming process. In fact, their collection consists of tweets in foreign languages. They use Google translate to convert it into English before the annotation process. Each tweet is labeled by a human annotator as *positive*, *negative*, *neutral* or *junk*. The "junk" label means that the tweet cannot be understood by a human annotator. A manual analysis of a random sample of tweets labeled as "junk" suggested that many of these tweets were those that were not translated well using Google translate. We eliminate the tweets with *junk* label for experiments. This leaves us with an unbalanced sample of 8,753 tweets. We use stratified sampling to get a balanced data-set of 5127 tweets (1709 tweets each from classes positive, negative and neutral).

4 Resources and Pre-processing of data

In this paper we introduce two new resources for pre-processing twitter data: 1) an emoticon dictionary and 2) an acronym dictionary. We prepare the emoticon dictionary by labeling 170 emoticons listed on Wikipedia[1] with their emotional state. For example, ":)" is labeled as positive whereas ":=(" is labeled as negative. We assign each emoticon a label from the following set of labels: Extremely-positive, Extremely-negative, Positive, Negative, and Neutral. We compile an acronym dictionary from an online resource.[2] The dictionary has translations for 5,184 acronyms. For example, *lol* is translated to *laughing out loud*.

We pre-process all the tweets as follows: a) replace all the emoticons with a their sentiment polarity by looking up the emoticon dictionary, b) replace all URLs with a tag $||U||$, c) replace targets (e.g. "@John") with tag $||T||$, d) replace all negations (e.g. *not*, *no*, *never*, *n't*, *cannot*) by tag "NOT", and e) replace a sequence of repeated characters by three characters, for example, convert *coooooooool* to *coool*. We do not replace the sequence by only two characters since we want to differentiate between the regular usage and emphasized usage of the word.

Acronym	English expansion
gr8, gr8t	great
lol	laughing out loud
rotf	rolling on the floor
bff	best friend forever

Table 1: Example acrynom and their expansion in the acronym dictionary.

We present some preliminary statistics about the data in Table 3. We use the Stanford tokenizer (Klein and Manning, 2003) to tokenize the tweets. We use a stop word dictionary[3] to identify stop words. All the other words which are found in WordNet (Fellbaum, 1998) are counted as English words. We use

[1] http://en.wikipedia.org/wiki/List_of_emoticons
[2] http://www.noslang.com/
[3] http://www.webconfs.com/stop-words.php

Emoticon	Polarity
:-) :) :o) :] :3 :c)	Positive
:D C:	Extremely-Positive
:-(:(:c :[	Negative
D8 D; D= DX v.v	Extremely-Negative
: |	Neutral

Table 2: Part of the dictionary of emoticons

the standard tagset defined by the Penn Treebank for identifying punctuation. We record the occurrence of three standard twitter tags: emoticons, URLs and targets. The remaining tokens are either non English words (like *coool*, *zzz* etc.) or other symbols.

Number of tokens	79,152
Number of stop words	30,371
Number of English words	23,837
Number of punctuation marks	9,356
Number of capitalized words	4,851
Number of twitter tags	3,371
Number of exclamation marks	2,228
Number of negations	942
Number of other tokens	9047

Table 3: Statistics about the data used for our experiments.

In Table 3 we see that 38.3% of the tokens are stop words, 30.1% of the tokens are found in WordNet and 1.2% tokens are negation words. 11.8% of all the tokens are punctuation marks excluding exclamation marks which make up for 2.8% of all tokens. In total, 84.1% of all tokens are tokens that we expect to see in a typical English language text. There are 4.2% tags that are specific to Twitter which include emoticons, target, hastags and "RT" (retweet). The remaining 11.7% tokens are either words that cannot be found in WordNet (like *Zzzzz*, *kewl*) or special symbols which do not fall in the category of Twitter tags.

5 Prior polarity scoring

A number of our features are based on prior polarity of words. For obtaining the prior polarity of words, we take motivation from work by Agarwal et al. (2009). We use Dictionary of Affect in Language (DAL) (Whissel, 1989) and extend it using WordNet. This dictionary of about 8000 English language words assigns every word a pleasantness score ($\in \mathbb{R}$) between 1 (Negative) - 3 (Positive). We first normalize the scores by diving each score my the scale (which is equal to 3). We consider words with polarity less than 0.5 as negative, higher than 0.8 as positive and the rest as neutral. If a word is not directly found in the dictionary, we retrieve all synonyms from Wordnet. We then look for each of the synonyms in DAL. If any synonym is found in DAL, we assign the original word the same pleasantness score as its synonym. If none of the synonyms is present in DAL, the word is not associated with any prior polarity. For the given data we directly found prior polarity of 81.1% of the words. We find polarity of other 7.8% of the words by using WordNet. So we find prior polarity of about 88.9% of English language words.

6 Design of Tree Kernel

We design a tree representation of tweets to combine many categories of features in one succinct convenient representation. For calculating the similarity between two trees we use a Partial Tree (PT) kernel first proposed by Moschitti (2006). A PT kernel calculates the similarity between two trees by comparing all possible sub-trees. This tree kernel is an instance of a general class of convolution kernels. Convolution Kernels, first introduced by Haussler (1999), can be used to compare abstract objects, like strings, instead of feature vectors. This is because these kernels involve a recursive calculation over the "parts" of abstract object. This calculation is made computationally efficient by using Dynamic Programming techniques. By considering all possible combinations of fragments, tree kernels capture any possible correlation between features and categories of features.

Figure 1 shows an example of the tree structure we design. This tree is for a synthesized tweet: *@Fernando this isn't a great day for playing the HARP! :)*. We use the following procedure to convert a tweet into a tree representation: Initialize the main tree to be "ROOT". Then tokenize each tweet and for each token: a) if the token is a target, emoticon, exclamation mark, other punctuation mark, or a negation word, add a leaf node to the "ROOT" with

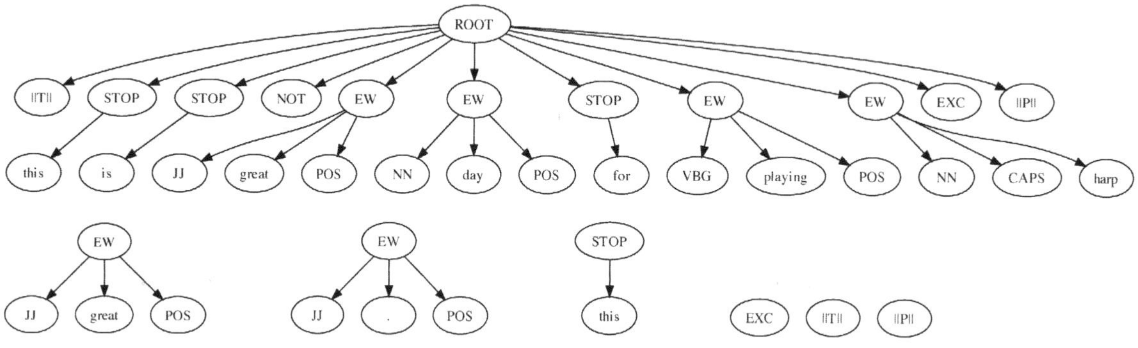

Figure 1: Tree kernel for a synthesized tweet: "@Fernando this isn't a great day for playing the HARP! :)"

the corresponding tag. For example, in the tree in Figure 1 we add tag $||T||$ (target) for "@Fernando", add tag "NOT" for the token "n't", add tag "EXC" for the exclamation mark at the end of the sentence and add $||P||$ for the emoticon representing positive mood. b) if the token is a stop word, we simply add the subtree " (STOP ('stop-word'))" to "ROOT". For instance, we add a subtree corresponding to each of the stop words: *this*, *is*, and *for*. c) if the token is an English language word, we map the word to its part-of-speech tag, calculate the prior polarity of the word using the procedure described in section 5 and add the subtree (EW ('POS' 'word' 'prior polarity')) to the "ROOT". For example, we add the subtree (EW (JJ great POS)) for the word *great*. "EW" refers to English word. d) For any other token <token> we add subtree "(NE (<token>))" to the "ROOT". "NE" refers to non-English.

The PT tree kernel creates all possible subtrees and compares them to each other. These subtrees include subtrees in which non-adjacent branches become adjacent by excising other branches, though order is preserved. In Figure 1, we show some of the tree fragments that the PT kernel will attempt to compare with tree fragments from other trees. For example, given the tree (EW (JJ) (great) (POS)), the PT kernel will use (EW (JJ) (great) (POS)), (EW (great) (POS)), (EW (JJ) (POS)), (EW (JJ) (great)), (EW (JJ)), (EW (great)), (EW (POS)), (EW), (JJ), (great), and (POS). This means that the PT tree kernel attempts to use full information, and also abstracts away from specific information (such as the lexical item). In this manner, it is not necessary to create by hand features at all levels of abstraction.

7 Our features

We propose a set of features listed in Table 4 for our experiments. These are a total of 50 type of features. We calculate these features for the whole tweet and for the last one-third of the tweet. In total we get 100 additional features. We refer to these features as Senti-features throughout the paper.

Our features can be divided into three broad categories: ones that are primarily counts of various features and therefore the value of the feature is a natural number $\in \mathbb{N}$. Second, features whose value is a real number $\in \mathbb{R}$. These are primarily features that capture the score retrieved from DAL. Thirdly, features whose values are boolean $\in \mathbb{B}$. These are bag of words, presence of exclamation marks and capitalized text. Each of these broad categories is divided into two subcategories: Polar features and Non-polar features. We refer to a feature as polar if we calculate its prior polarity either by looking it up in DAL (extended through WordNet) or in the emoticon dictionary. All other features which are not associated with any prior polarity fall in the Non-polar category. Each of Polar and Non-polar features is further subdivided into two categories: POS and Other. POS refers to features that capture statistics about parts-of-speech of words and Other refers to all other types of features.

In reference to Table 4, row f_1 belongs to the category Polar POS and refers to the count of number of positive and negative parts-of-speech (POS) in a tweet, rows f_2, f_3, f_4 belongs to the category Polar Other and refers to count of number of negation words, count of words that have positive and negative prior polarity, count of emoticons per polarity type, count of hashtags, capitalized words and words with exclamation marks associated with words that have prior polarity, row f_5 belongs to the category Non-Polar POS and refers to counts of different parts-of-speech tags, rows f_6, f_7 belong to the category Non-Polar Other and refer to count of number of slangs, latin alphabets, and other words without polarity. It also relates to special terms such as the number of hashtags, URLs, targets and newlines. Row f_8 belongs to the category Polar POS and captures the summation of prior polarity scores of words with POS of JJ, RB, VB and NN. Similarly, row f_9 belongs to the category Polar Other and calculates the summation of prior polarity scores of all words, row f_{10} refers to the category Non-Polar Other and calculates the percentage of tweet that is capitalized.

Finally, row f_{11} belongs to the category Non-Polar Other and refers to presence of exclamation and presence of capitalized words as features.

8 Experiments and Results

In this section, we present experiments and results for two classification tasks: 1) Positive versus Negative and 2) Positive versus Negative versus Neutral. For each of the classification tasks we present three models, as well as results for two combinations of these models:

1. Unigram model (our baseline)
2. Tree kernel model
3. 100 Senti-features model
4. Kernel plus Senti-features
5. Unigram plus Senti-features

For the unigram plus Senti-features model, we present feature analysis to gain insight about what kinds of features are adding most value to the model. We also present learning curves for each of the models and compare learning abilities of models when provided limited data.

Experimental-Set-up: For all our experiments we use Support Vector Machines (SVM) and report averaged 5-fold cross-validation test results. We tune the C parameter for SVM using an embedded 5-fold cross-validation on the training data of each fold, i.e. for each fold, we first run 5-fold cross-validation only on the training data of that fold for different values of C. We pick the setting that yields the best cross-validation error and use that C for determining test error for that fold. As usual, the reported accuracies is the average over the five folds.

8.1 Positive versus Negative

This is a binary classification task with two classes of sentiment polarity: positive and negative. We use a balanced data-set of 1709 instances for each class and therefore the chance baseline is 50%.

8.1.1 Comparison of models

We use a unigram model as our baseline. Researchers report state-of-the-art performance for sentiment analysis on Twitter data using a unigram model (Go et al., 2009; Pak and Paroubek, 2010). Table 5 compares the performance of three models: unigram model, feature based model using only 100 Senti-features, and the tree kernel model. We report mean and standard deviation of 5-fold test accuracy. We observe that the tree kernels outperform the unigram and the Senti-features by 2.58% and 2.66% respectively. The 100 Senti-features described in Table 4 performs as well as the unigram model that uses about 10,000 features. We also experiment with combination of models. Combining unigrams with Senti-features outperforms the combination of kernels with Senti-features by 0.78%. This is our best performing system for the positive versus negative task, gaining about 4.04% absolute gain over a hard unigram baseline.

8.1.2 Feature Analysis

Table 6 presents classifier accuracy and F1-measure when features are added incrementally. We start with our baseline unigram model and subsequently add various sets of features. First, we add all non-polar features (rows $f_5, f_6, f_7, f_{10}, f_{11}$ in Table 4) and observe no improvement in the performance. Next, we add all part-of-speech based features (rows f_1, f_8) and observe a gain of 3.49% over the unigram baseline. We see an additional increase in accuracy by 0.55% when we add other prior polarity features (rows f_2, f_3, f_4, f_9 in Table 4). From

$\mathbb{N}$	Polar	POS	# of (+/-) POS (JJ, RB, VB, NN)	f_1
		Other	# of negation words, positive words, negative words	f_2
			# of extremely-pos., extremely-neg., positive, negative emoticons	f_3
			# of (+/-) hashtags, capitalized words, exclamation words	f_4
	Non-Polar	POS	# of JJ, RB, VB, NN	f_5
		Other	# of slangs, latin alphabets, dictionary words, words	f_6
			# of hashtags, URLs, targets, newlines	f_7
$\mathbb{R}$	Polar	POS	For POS JJ, RB, VB, NN, $\sum$ prior pol. scores of words of that POS	f_8
		Other	$\sum$ prior polarity scores of all words	f_9
	Non-Polar	Other	percentage of capitalized text	f_{10}
$\mathbb{B}$	Non-Polar	Other	exclamation, capitalized text	f_{11}

Table 4: $\mathbb{N}$ refers to set of features whose value is a positive integer. They are primarily count features; for example, count of number of positive adverbs, negative verbs etc. $\mathbb{R}$ refers to features whose value is a real number; for example, sum of the prior polarity scores of words with part-of-speech of adjective/adverb/verb/noun, and sum of prior polarity scores of all words. $\mathbb{B}$ refers to the set of features that have a boolean value; for example, presence of exclamation marks, presence of capitalized text.

Model	Avg. Acc (%)	Std. Dev. (%)
Unigram	71.35	1.95
Senti-features	71.27	0.65
Kernel	**73.93**	1.50
Unigram + Senti-features	**75.39**	1.29
Kernel + Senti-features	74.61	1.43

Table 5: Average and standard deviation for test accuracy for the 2-way classification task using different models: Unigram (baseline), tree kernel, Senti-features, unigram plus Senti-features, and tree kernel plus senti-features.

Features	Acc.	F1 Measure	
		Pos	Neg
Unigram baseline	71.35	71.13	71.50
+ $f_5, f_6, f_7, f_{10}, f_{11}$	70.1	69.66	70.46
+ f_1, f_8	74.84	74.4	75.2
+ f_2, f_3, f_4, f_9	**75.39**	74.81	75.86

Table 6: Accuracy and F1-measure for 2-way classification task using Unigrams and Senti-features. All f_i refer to Table 4 and are cumulative.

Positive words	love, great, good, thanks
Negative words	hate, shit, hell, tired
Emoticons	$\|\|P\|\|$ (positive emoticon), $\|\|N\|\|$ (negative emoticon)
Other	for, $\|\|U\|\|$ (URL)

Table 7: List of top unigram features for 2-way task.

these experiments we conclude that the most important features in Senti-features are those that involve prior polarity of parts-of-speech. All other features play a marginal role in achieving the best performing system. In fact, we experimented by using unigrams with only prior polarity POS features and achieved a performance of 75.1%, which is only slightly lower than using all Senti-features.

In terms of unigram features, we use Information Gain as the attribute evaluation metric to do feature selection. In Table 7 we present a list of unigrams that consistently appear as top 15 unigram features across all folds. Words having positive or negative prior polarity top the list. Emoticons also appear as important unigrams. Surprisingly though, the word *for* appeared as a top feature. A preliminary analysis revealed that the word *for* appears as frequently in positive tweets as it does in negative tweets. However, tweets containing phrases like *for you* and *for me* tend to be positive even in the absence of any other explicit prior polarity words. Owing to previous research, the URL appearing as a top feature is less surprising because Go et al. (2009) report that tweets containing URLs tend to be positive.

8.1.3 Learning curve

The learning curve for the 2-way classification task is in Figure 2. The curve shows that when lim-

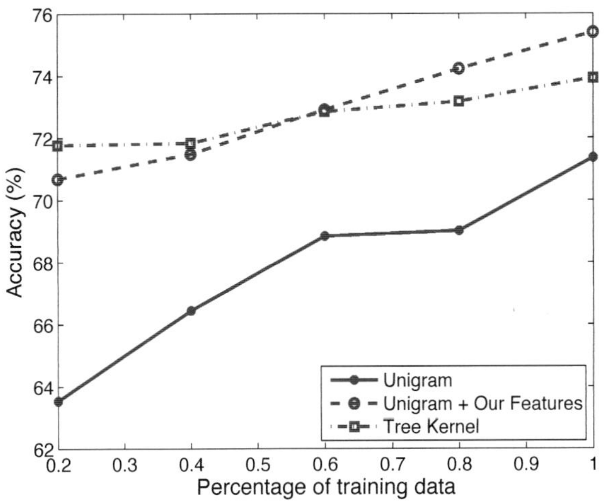

Figure 2: Learning curve for two-way classification task.

ited data is used the advantages in the performance of our best performing systems is even more pronounced. This implies that with limited amount of training data, simply using unigrams has a critical disadvantage, while both tree kernel and unigram model with our features exhibit promising performance.

8.2 Positive versus Negative versus Neutral

This is a 3-way classification task with classes of sentiment polarity: positive, negative and neutral. We use a balanced data-set of 1709 instances for each class and therefore the chance baseline is 33.33%.

8.2.1 Comparison of models

For this task the unigram model achieves a gain of 23.25% over chance baseline. Table 8 compares the performance of our three models. We report mean and standard deviation of 5-fold test accuracy. We observe that the tree kernels outperform the unigram and the Senti-features model by 4.02% and 4.29% absolute, respectively. We note that this difference is much more pronounced comparing to the two way classification task. Once again, our 100 Senti-features perform almost as well as the unigram baseline which has about 13,000 features. We also experiment with the combination of models. For this classification task the combination of tree kernel with Senti-features outperforms the combination of unigrams with Senti-features by a small margin.

Model	Avg. Acc (%)	Std. Dev. (%)
Unigram	56.58	1.52
Senti-features	56.31	0.69
Kernel	**60.60**	1.00
Unigram + Senti-features	60.50	2.27
Kernel + Senti-features	**60.83**	1.09

Table 8: Average and standard deviation for test accuracy for the 3-way classification task using different models: Unigram (baseline), tree kernel, Senti-features, unigram plus Senti-features, and Senti-features plus tree kernels.

This is our best performing system for the 3-way classification task, gaining 4.25% over the unigram baseline.

The learning curve for the 3-way classification task is similar to the curve of the 2-way classification task, and we omit it.

8.2.2 Feature Analysis

Table 9 presents classifier accuracy and F1-measure when features are added incrementally. We start with our baseline unigram model and subsequently add various sets of features. First, we add all non-polar features (rows f_5, f_6, f_7, f_{10} in Table 4) and observe an small improvement in the performance. Next, we add all part-of-speech based features and observe a gain of 3.28% over the unigram baseline. We see an additional increase in accuracy by 0.64% when we add other prior polarity features (rows f_2, f_3, f_4, f_9 in Table 4). These results are in line with our observations for the 2-way classification task. Once again, the main contribution comes from features that involve prior polarity of parts-of-speech.

Features	Acc.	F1 Measure		
		Pos	Neu	Neg
Unigram baseline	56.58	56.86	56.58	56.20
+ $f_5, f_6, f_7, f_{10}, f_{11}$	56.91	55.12	59.84	55
+ f_1, f_8	59.86	58.42	61.04	59.82
+ f_2, f_3, f_4, f_9	**60.50**	59.41	60.15	61.86

Table 9: Accuracy and F1-measure for 3-way classification task using unigrams and Senti-features.

The top ranked unigram features for the 3-way

classification task are mostly similar to that of the 2-way classification task, except several terms with neutral polarity appear to be discriminative features, such as *to*, *have*, and *so*.

9 Conclusion

We presented results for sentiment analysis on Twitter. We use previously proposed state-of-the-art unigram model as our baseline and report an overall gain of over 4% for two classification tasks: a binary, positive versus negative and a 3-way positive versus negative versus neutral. We presented a comprehensive set of experiments for both these tasks on manually annotated data that is a random sample of stream of tweets. We investigated two kinds of models: tree kernel and feature based models and demonstrate that both these models outperform the unigram baseline. For our feature-based approach, we do feature analysis which reveals that the most important features are those that combine the prior polarity of words and their parts-of-speech tags. We tentatively conclude that sentiment analysis for Twitter data is not that different from sentiment analysis for other genres.

In future work, we will explore even richer linguistic analysis, for example, parsing, semantic analysis and topic modeling.

10 Acknowledgments

Agarwal and Rambow are funded by NSF grant IIS-0713548. Vovsha is funded by NSF grant IIS-0916200. We would like to thank NextGen Invent (NGI) Corporation for providing us with the Twitter data. Please contact Deepak Mittal (deepak.mittal@ngicorportion.com) about obtaining the data.

References

Apoorv Agarwal, Fadi Biadsy, and Kathleen Mckeown. 2009. Contextual phrase-level polarity analysis using lexical affect scoring and syntactic n-grams. *Proceedings of the 12th Conference of the European Chapter of the ACL (EACL 2009)*, pages 24–32, March.

Luciano Barbosa and Junlan Feng. 2010. Robust sentiment detection on twitter from biased and noisy data. *Proceedings of the 23rd International Conference on Computational Linguistics: Posters*, pages 36–44.

Adam Bermingham and Alan Smeaton. 2010. Classifying sentiment in microblogs: is brevity an advantage is brevity an advantage? *ACM*, pages 1833–1836.

C. Fellbaum. 1998. *Wordnet, an electronic lexical database*. MIT Press.

Michael Gamon. 2004. Sentiment classification on customer feedback data: noisy data, large feature vectors, and the role of linguistic analysis. *Proceedings of the 20th international conference on Computational Linguistics*.

Alec Go, Richa Bhayani, and Lei Huang. 2009. Twitter sentiment classification using distant supervision. Technical report, Stanford.

David Haussler. 1999. Convolution kernels on discrete structures. Technical report, University of California at Santa Cruz.

M Hu and B Liu. 2004. Mining and summarizing customer reviews. *KDD*.

S M Kim and E Hovy. 2004. Determining the sentiment of opinions. *Coling*.

Dan Klein and Christopher D. Manning. 2003. Accurate unlexicalized parsing. *Proceedings of the 41st Meeting of the Association for Computational Linguistics*, pages 423–430.

Alessandro Moschitti. 2006. Efficient convolution kernels for dependency and constituent syntactic trees. In *Proceedings of the 17th European Conference on Machine Learning*.

Alexander Pak and Patrick Paroubek. 2010. Twitter as a corpus for sentiment analysis and opinion mining. *Proceedings of LREC*.

B. Pang and L. Lee. 2004. A sentimental education: Sentiment analysis using subjectivity analysis using subjectivity summarization based on minimum cuts. *ACL*.

P. Turney. 2002. Thumbs up or thumbs down? semantic orientation applied to unsupervised classification of reviews. *ACL*.

C M Whissel. 1989. *The dictionary of Affect in Language*. Emotion: theory research and experience, Acad press London.

T. Wilson, J. Wiebe, and P. Hoffman. 2005. Recognizing contextual polarity in phrase level sentiment analysis. *ACL*.

Detecting Forum Authority Claims in Online Discussions

Alex Marin, Bin Zhang, Mari Ostendorf
Department of Electrical Engineering
University of Washington
{amarin, binz}@uw.edu, mo@ee.washington.edu

Abstract

This paper explores the problem of detecting sentence-level forum authority claims in online discussions. Using a maximum entropy model, we explore a variety of strategies for extracting lexical features in a sparse training scenario, comparing knowledge- and data-driven methods (and combinations). The augmentation of lexical features with parse context is also investigated. We find that certain markup features perform remarkably well alone, but are outperformed by data-driven selection of lexical features augmented with parse context.

1 Introduction

In multi-party discussions, language is used to establish identity, status, authority and connections with others in addition to communicating information and opinions. Automatically extracting this type of social information in language from discussions is useful for understanding group interactions and relationships.

The aspect of social communication most explored so far is the detection of participant role, particularly in spoken genres such as broadcast news, broadcast conversations, and meetings. Several studies have explored different types of features (lexical, prosodic, and turn-taking) in a variety of statistical modeling frameworks (Barzilay et al., 2000; Maskey and Hirschberg, 2006; Liu, 2006; Liu and Liu, 2007; Vinciarelli, 2007; Laskowski et al., 2008; Hutchinson et al., 2010). Typically, these studies assume that a speaker inhabits a role for the duration of the discussion, so multiple turns contribute to the decision. Participant status is similar although the language of others is often more relevant than that of the participant in question.

Communication of other types of social information can be more localized. For example, an attempt to establish authority frequently occurs within a single sentence or turn when entering a discussion, though authority bids may involve multiple turns when the participant is challenged. Similarly, discussion participants may align with or distance themselves from other participants with a single statement, or someone could agree with one person at a particular point in the conversation and disagree with them at a different point. Such localized phenomena are also important for understanding the broader context of that participant's influence or role in the conversation (Bunderson, 2003).

In this paper, we focus on a particular type of authority claim, namely forum claims, as defined in a companion paper (Bender et al., 2011). Forum claims are based on policy, norms, or contextual rules of behavior in the interaction. In our experiments, we explore the phenomenon using Wikipedia discussion ("talk") pages, which are discussions associated with a Wikipedia article in which changes to the article are debated by the editors in a series of discussion threads. Examples of such forum claims are:

- *I do think my understanding of Wikipedia and policy is better than yours.*
- *So it has all those things going for it, and I do think it complies with [[WP:V]] and*

[[WP:WTA]].

- *Folks, please be specific and accurate when you [[WP:CITE—cite your sources]].*

We treat each discussion thread as a unique "conversation". Each contiguous change to a conversation is treated as a unique "post" or turn. The dataset and annotation scheme are described in more detail in the companion paper.

Related previous work on a similar task focused on detecting attempts to establish topic expertise in Wikipedia discussions (Marin et al., 2010). Their work used a different annotation process than that which we build on here. In particular, the annotation was performed at the discussion participant level, with evidence marked at the turn level without distinguishing the different types of claims as in (Bender et al., 2011).

Treating the problem of detecting forum claims as a sentence-level classification problem is similar to other natural language processing tasks, such as sentiment classification. Early work in sentiment analysis used unigram features (Pang and Lee, 2004; Pang and Lee, 2005). However, error analyses suggested that highly accurate sentiment classification requires deeper understanding of the text, or at least higher order n-gram features. Kim and Hovy (2006) used unigrams, bigrams, and trigrams for extracting the polarity of online reviews. Gilbert et al. (2009) employed weighted n-grams together with additional features to classify blog comments based on agreement polarity. We conjecture that authority claim detection will also benefit from moving beyond unigram features.

The focus of the paper is on two questions in feature extraction:

- Can we exploit domain knowledge to address overtraining issues in sparse data conditions?
- Is parse context more effective than n-gram context?

Our experiments compare the performance obtained using multiple methods for incorporating linguistic- or data-driven knowledge and context into the feature space, relative to the baseline n-gram features. Section 2 describes the general classification architecture. Section 3 describes the various features implemented. Experimental results are presented in section 4. We conclude with some analysis in section 5 and remarks on future work in section 6.

2 System Description

We implement a classification system that assigns a binary label to each sentence in a conversation, indicating whether or not a forum authority claim is being made in that sentence. To obtain higher-level decisions, we apply a simple rule that any post which contains at least one sentence-level forum authority claim should be labeled positive. We use the sentence-level system to obtain turn-level (post-level) decisions instead of training directly on the higher-level data units because the forum claims are relatively infrequent events. Thus, we believe that the classification using localized features will yield better results; when using higher-level classification units, the positive phenomena would be overwhelmed by the negative features in the rest of the sample, leading to poorer performance.

Given a potentially large class imbalance due to the sparsity of the positive-labeled samples, tuning on accuracy scores would lead to very low recall. Thus, we tune and evaluate on F-score, defined as the harmonic mean of precision (the percent of detected claims that are correct) and recall (the percent of true claims that are detected).

The classifier used is a maximum entropy classifier (MaxEnt), implemented using the MALLET package (McCallum, 2002), an open-source java implementation. MaxEnt models the conditional probability distribution $p(c|\mathbf{x})$ of a forum claim c given the feature vector $\mathbf{x}$ in a log-linear form. Model parameters $\lambda_i^{(c)}$ are estimated using gradient descent on the training data log likelihood with L2 regularization.

Since our task is a two-class problem, and the objective is the F-score, we use a classification decision with decision threshold θ, i.e.

$$c^* = \begin{cases} \text{true} & \text{if } p(\text{true}|\mathbf{x}) > \theta, \\ \text{false} & \text{otherwise.} \end{cases}$$

where θ is tuned on the development set, and the optimal value is usually found to be much smaller than 0.5.

3 Features

Past work on various NLP tasks has shown that lexical features can be quite effective in categorizing linguistic phenomena. However, using a large number of features when the number of labeled training samples is small often leads to overtraining, due to the *curse of dimensionality* when dealing with high-dimensional feature spaces (Hastie et al., 2009). Thus, we investigate two task-dependent methods for generating lexical feature lists: a combined data- and knowledge-driven method using related Wikipedia content, and a knowledge-driven method requiring manual feature list generation.

We conjecture that using unigram features alone is often insufficient to capture the more complex phenomena associated with the forum claim detection task. Empirically, we find that even the word features most strongly correlated with the class variable are frequent in both classes. In particular, due to the class imbalance, such features are often more prevalent in the negative class samples than the positive class samples. We believe that additional information about the context in which such words appear in the data could be relevant for further increasing their discriminative power.

One method often used in the literature to capture the context in which a particular word appears is to define the context as its neighboring words, e.g. by using higher-order n-grams (such as bigrams or trigrams) or phrase patterns. However, this method also suffers from the *curse of dimensionality* problem, as seen from the feature set size increase for our training set when moving beyond unigrams (listed in table 1.)

Features	Counts
Unigrams	13,899
Bigrams	109,449
Trigrams	211,580

Table 1: N-gram feature statistics

To understand the meaning of a sentence, features based only on surface word forms may not be sufficient. We propose an alternate method that augments each word with information from the structure of a parse tree for each sentence in which that word appears.

Additionally, we use a small set of other (non-lexical) features, motivated by anecdotal examples from Wikipedia discussions.

3.1 Generating Word Feature Lists

We propose two knowledge-assisted methods for selecting lexical features, as described below, both of which are combined with data-driven selection of the most discriminative features based on mutual information.

3.1.1 Leveraging "Parallel" Data

The Wikipedia data naturally has "parallel" data in that each talk page is associated with an article, and there are additional pages that describe forum policies and norms of behavior. By comparing article and talk pages, one can extract words that tend to be associated with editor discussions (words which have high TF-IDF in a discussion but low TF-IDF in the associated article). By comparing to the policies pages, one can identify words that are likely to be used in policy-related forum claims (words with high average TF-IDF in the corpus of policy and norms of behavior pages.) To select a single reduced set of words, we pick only the words with sufficiently high TF-IDF in the discussion pages. In practice, to avoid tuning additional parameters, we selected the settings which yielded the largest list (with approximately 520 words) and let the feature selection process trim down the list. Some words identified by the feature selection process include:

- words shared with the knowledge-driven list (discussed below): *wikipedia, policy, sources, guidelines, reliable, rules, please*
- relevant words not appearing in the knowledge-driven list: *categories, pages, article, wiki, editing*
- other words: *was, not, who, is, see*

3.1.2 Knowledge-Driven Word List

The knowledge-driven method uses lists of words picked by trained linguists who developed the guidelines for the process of annotating our dataset. Six lists were developed, containing keywords and short phrases related to:

- behavior in discussion forums (*reliable, respectful, balanced, unacceptable*)
- politeness (*please, would you, could you, would you mind*)
- positioning and expressing neutrality (*point of view, neutral, opinion, bias, good faith*)
- accepted practices in discussion forums (*practice, custom, conflict, consensus*)
- sourcing information (*source, citing, rules, policy, original research*)
- Wikipedia-specific keywords (*wikipedia, administrator, registered, unregistered*)

In all our experiments, the various word lists were concatenated and used as a single set of 75 words. Phrases were treated as single keywords for purposes of feature extraction, i.e. a single feature was extracted for each phrase. If another word on the list were a substring of a given phrase, and the phrase were found to appear in the text of a given sample, both the single word and the phrase were kept in that sample.

3.2 Adding Higher-Level Linguistic Context

As an alternative to using n-grams as lexical context, we propose using syntactic context, represented by information about the parse tree of each sentence in the data. Given the low amount of available training data, learning n-gram features we believe is likely to overtrain, due to the combinatorial explosion in the feature space. On the other hand, adding parse tree context information to each feature results in a much smaller increase in feature space, due to the smaller number of non-terminal tokens as compared to the vocabulary size. To extract such features, the data was run through a version of the Berkeley parser (Petrov et al., 2006) trained on the Wall Street Journal portion of the Penn Treebank.

For each sentence, the one-best parse was used to extract the list of non-terminals above each word in the sequence. The list was then filtered to a shorter subset of non-terminal tags. The words augmented with non-terminal parse tree tags were treated as individual features and used in the usual way. We used a context of at most three non-terminal tags (i.e. the POS tag and two additional levels if present.)

For simplicity, multi-word phrases from the knowledge-driven word list were either removed entirely, or split with each word augmented independently. Using this method resulted in the feature counts shown in table 2. In particular, we see that splitting phrases instead of removing them results in almost twice as many parse-augmented word features, in great part due to function words appearing in a variety of unrelated contexts.

Features	Counts
All unigrams	38,384
Data-driven list	5,935
Knowledge-driven list, no phrases	504
Knowledge-driven list, split phrases	908

Table 2: Parse feature statistics

3.3 Other Features

We use a number of additional features not directly related to lexical cues. We extract the following sentence complexity features:

- the length of the sentence
- the average length of the 20% longest words in the sentence

Additionally, we use a number of other features motivated by our analysis of the data. These features are:

- the number of words containing only uppercase letters in that sentence
- the number of (external) URLs in the sentence
- the number of links to Wikipedia pages containing norms of forum behavior or policies
- the number of other Wikipedia-internal links

4 Experiments

4.1 Dataset and Procedure

We use data from the Authority and Alignment in Wikipedia Discussions (AAWD) corpus described in our companion paper (Bender et al., 2011). The dataset contains English Wikipedia discussions annotated with authority claims by four annotators. Not all the discussions are annotated by multiple annotators. Thereby in the train/dev/eval split, we select most of the discussions that are multiply annotated for the dev and eval sets. The statistics of each set are shown in table 3.

	Train	Dev	Eval
# files	226	56	55
# sentences	17512	4990	4200

Table 3: Data statistics

A number of experiments were conducted to assess the performance of the various feature types proposed. We evaluate the effect of individual features when used in a MaxEnt classifier, as well as combined features.

We tune the number of features selected by the mutual information between a feature and the class labels, which is a common approach applied in text categorization (Yang and Pedersen, 1997). Feature selection and parameter tuning of the decision threshold θ are performed independently for each condition. We include the number of features selected in each case alongside the results. The performance of the various systems described in this paper is evaluated using F-score. The numbers corresponding to the overall best performance obtained on the dev and eval sets are highlighted in boldface in the appropriate table.

4.2 N-gram Features

First, we examine the performance of lexical features extracted at different n-gram lengths. We used maximum n-gram sizes 1, 2, and 3, and the counts of n-grams were used as features for MaxEnt. The results are summarized in table 4.

Maximum n-gram length	# selected features	Dev	Eval
1	50	0.321	0.270
2	50	0.331	0.300
3	20	0.333	0.290

Table 4: N-gram feature results

4.3 "Smart" Word Features

The second set of experiments compares the performance of various methods of selecting unigram lexical features. We compare using the full vocabulary with the two selection methods, outlined in section 3.1. The combination of the two simpler selection methods was also examined, under the assumption that the parallel-data-driven features may be more complete, but also more likely to overtrain, since they were derived directly from the data. The results are summarized in table 5.

Feature	# selected features	Dev	Eval
All words	50	0.321	0.270
Parallel corpus words	10	0.281	0.231
Hand-picked words	50	0.340	0.272
Parallel corpus + hand-picked words	100	0.303	0.259

Table 5: Smart word feature results

4.4 Parse-Augmented Features

A third set of experiments examines the effect of adding parsing-related context to the features. We use the same set of features as in section 3.2. For the knowledge-driven features, we present both versions of the parse features, the one in which phrases were split into their constituent words before augmentation with parse features, and the one from which phrases were removed altogether. The results are summarized in table 6.

Word list to derive features from	# selected features	Dev	Eval
All words	50	0.352	0.445
Parallel corpus words	20	0.336	0.433
Hand-picked words (no phrases)	50	0.314	0.306
Hand-picked words (split phrases)	50	0.328	0.310
Parallel corpus + hand-picked words (no phrases)	50	0.367	0.457
Parallel corpus + hand-picked words (split phrases)	50	0.359	0.450

Table 6: Parse-augmented feature results

We perform a small empirical analysis of features in the model with parse-augmented features for all words. Table 7 contains some of the most common features, their counts for each class, and model weight (if selected.) As expected, the feature with the highest relative frequency in the positive class gets the highest model weight. Other features with high absolute frequency in the positive class also get some positive weight. All other features are discarded during model training.

Feature	# false	# true	Weight
Wikipedia_NNP_NP_PP	60	10	1.035
Wikipedia_NNP_NP_S	57	12	1.121
Wikipedia_NNP_NP_NP	26	16	1.209
Wikipedia_NNP_NP_VP	13	3	-
Wikipedia_JJ_NP_NP	6	0	-
Wikipedia_NNP_NP_FRAG	1	3	2.115

Table 7: Parse feature examples

4.5 Other Features

A fourth set of experiments shows the effect of Wikipedia-specific markup features described in Section 4.5. The results for the Wikipedia policy page feature are listed in table 8. The other features were found to not be useful, resulting in F-scores of less than 0.1.

Feature	Dev	Eval
Wikipedia policy page	0.341	0.622

Table 8: Other feature results

4.6 Combined Features

The previous sets of experiments reveal that the feature of links to Wikipedia policy page is the most discriminative individual feature. Therefore, in the next set of experiments, we combine other features with the Wikipedia policy page feature to train MaxEnt models. We did not include any of the other features whose results were summarized in section 4.5, due to their very low individual performance. The results are shown in table 9.

Features other than Wikipedia policy page markup	# selected features	Dev	Eval
N-gram features			
unigram	20	0.448	0.550
unigram + bigram	50	0.447	0.551
unigram + bigram + trigram	100	0.446	0.596
Smart word features			
Parallel corpus words	20	0.427	0.483
Hand-picked words	50	**0.468**	0.596
Parallel corpus + hand-picked	100	0.451	0.569
Parse-augmented features			
All words	50	0.398	0.610
Parallel corpus words	100	0.381	0.623
Hand-picked words (no phrases)	20	0.392	**0.632**
Hand-picked words (split phrases)	100	0.392	0.558
Parallel corpus + hand-picked words (no phrases)	50	0.400	0.596
Parallel corpus + hand-picked words (split phrases)	50	0.398	0.607

Table 9: Combined feature results

4.7 Turn-level Classification

We propagate the sentence-level classification output to the turn-level if that turn has at least one sentence classified as forum claim. For simplicity, instead of running experiments on all the feature configurations, we use only the one that provides the highest dev set F-score, which is the MaxEnt classifier with Wikipedia policy page markup and hand-picked keyword features combined. The resulting F-score is 0.57 for the development set and 0.66 for the evaluation set.

5 Discussion

5.1 Data Variability

One of the most notable observations in the experiments above is the high degree of data variability. A simple rule-based classifier that uses only the Wikipedia policy page markup feature gives the best results on the evaluation set, but it is not nearly as effective on the development set. Simply put, the markup is a reliable cue when it is available, but it is not always present. Table 10 demonstrates this through the precision and recall results of the dev and eval sets. The variability also extends to the utility of parse features.

	Dev	Eval
Precision	0.703	0.862
Recall	0.225	0.487

Table 10: Precision and recall of the rule-based system

To better understand this issue, we reran the best case configurations on the dev and eval sets with the role of the dev and eval sets reversed, i.e. using the eval set for feature selection. For the best case configuration on the dev set (Wikipedia policy page markup and hand-picked keywords), 50 and 20 features are selected when tuned on dev and eval sets, respectively, and the latter feature set is a subset of the former one. For the best case configuration on the eval set (Wikipedia policy page markup and parse-augmented features derived from hand-picked words without phrases), the same 20 features are selected when tuned on dev or eval sets. For each configuration, the combined feature set from the two different selection experiments was then used to train a new model, which was evaluated on the combined dev and eval test sets. The precision/recall trade-off is illustrated in figure 1, which can be compared to a precision of 0.78 and recall of 0.32 using the rule-based system on the two test sets combined. While this is a "cheating experiment" in that the test data was used in feature selection, it gives a better idea of the potential gain from parse-augmented lexical features for this task. From the figure, both best-case configurations outperform the rule-based system, and an operating point with more balanced precision and recall can be chosen. Furthermore, the system with parse-augmented features is able to operate at a high recall while still maintaining reasonable precision, which is desirable in some applications.

5.2 Feature Analysis

The variability of data in this task poses challenges for learning features that improve over a simple knowledge-driven baseline. However, the results in section 4 provide some insights.

First, unigram features alone provide poor performance. Adding bigrams improves the performance on both the development and the evaluation sets, while further adding trigrams degrades the eval set performance. This indicates that there are some discriminative high-order n-grams, but also too many noisy n-grams to extract the discriminative n-grams effectively with a small amount of training data.

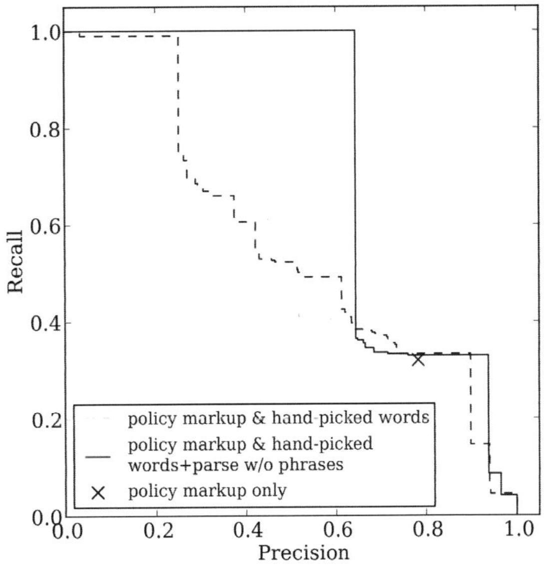

Figure 1: Precision-recall curve

The smarter word features do not perform as well as n-gram features when used alone (i.e. as unigrams), but they provide an improvement over n-grams when used with parse features. With parse features, the parallel corpus words are more effective than the hand-picked words, but the best performance is achieved with the combination. When combined with the Wikipedia policy page markup features, the hand-picked words are the most useful, with the best eval set results obained with the parse-augmented version.

Overall, the best performance seems to be obtained by using the combined feature set of Wikipedia policy page markup and hand-picked keyword features with parse augmentation. However, the test set variability discussed in section 5.1 suggests that it would be useful to assess the findings on additional data.

5.3 Further Challenges

By definition, a forum authority claim is composed of a mention of Wikipedia norms and policies to support a previously-mentioned opinion proposed by the participant. While the detection of mentions of Wikipedia norms is relatively easy, we conjecture that part of the difficulty of this task lies in identifying whether a mention of Wikipedia norms is for the purpose of supporting an opinion, or just a mention as part of the general conversation. For example, the Wikipedia policy *neutral point of view (NPOV)* is a frequently used term in talk pages. It can be used as support for the participant's suggested modification, or it can be just a mention of the policy without the purpose of supporting any opinion. For example, the sentence *This section should be deleted because it violates NPOV* is a forum claim, because the term *NPOV* is used to support the participant's request. However, the sentence *Thank you for removing the NPOV tag* is not a forum claim, as the participant is not presenting any opinion. For these reasons, the word *NPOV* alone does not provide enough information for reliable decisions; contextual information, such as n-grams and parse-augmented features, must be explored. On the other hand, a direct reference to a Wikipedia policy page is much less ambiguous, as it is almost always used in the context of strengthening an opinion or claim.

Another factor that makes the task challenging is the sparsity of the data. It is time-consuming to produce high quality annotations for forum claims, as many claims are subtle and therefore difficult to detect, even by human annotators. Given the limited amount of data, many features have low occurrences and cannot be learned properly. The data sparsity is an even bigger problem when the feature space is increased, for example by using contextual features such as n-grams and parse-augmented words. On the other hand, while it may be easier to capture the mention of Wikipedia policies using a limited set of keywords or phrases, it is difficult to model the behavior of presenting an opinion when the data is sparse, as the following forum claim examples show:

- *I think we can all agree that this issue bears mentioning, however the blurb as it stands is decidedly not NPOV, nor does it fit the formatting guidelines for a Wikipedia article.*
- *As a reminder, the threshold for inclusion in Wikipedia is whether material is attributable to a reliable published source, not whether it is true.*
- *If you think that some editor is violating NPOV, you can pursue dispute resolution, but it's no justification for moving or removing valid information.*
- *If you'd like to talk the position that quotes from people's opinions do not belong here, fine, but it is extremely POV to insist only on eliminating editorials that you disagree with, while not challenging quotes from your own POV.*

The examples above require deeper understanding of the sentences to identify the embedding of opinions. Modeling such phenomena using word-based contextual features when the training data is sparse is particularly hard. Even with parse-augmented features that do not increase the feature dimensionality as fast as n-grams, a certain amount of data is needed to obtain reliable statistics. Clustering of the features into a lower dimensional space would provide one possible solution to this issue, but how the clustering can be done robustly remains an open question.

6 Conclusions

We have presented systems to detect forum authority claims, which are claims of credibility using forum norms, in Wikipedia talk pages. The Wikipedia policy page markup feature was found to be the most effective individual feature for this task. We have also developed approaches to further improve the performance by knowledge-driven selection of lexical features and adding context in the form of parse information.

Future work includes extending the contextual features, such as parse-augmented word features, to other types of linguistic information, and automatically learning the types of contexts that might be most useful for each word. Feature clustering methods will also be investigated, in order to reduce feature space dimensionality and deal with data sparsity. To improve the effectiveness of the parse features, domain adaptation of the parser or use of a parser trained on data closer matched to our target domain could be investigated. We will also plan to extend this work to other types of authority claims in

Wikipedia and to other multi-party discussion genres.

Acknowledgments

This research was funded by the Office of the Director of National Intelligence (ODNI), Intelligence Advanced Research Projects Activity (IARPA). All statements of fact, opinion or conclusions contained herein are those of the authors and should not be construed as representing the official views or policies of IARPA, the ODNI or the U.S. Government.

References

R. Barzilay, M. Collins, J. Hirschberg, and S. Whittaker. 2000. The rules behind roles: Identifying speaker role in radio broadcasts. In *Proceedings of AAAI*, pages 679–684.

E. M. Bender, J. Morgan, M. Oxley, M. Zachry, B. Hutchinson, A. Marin, B. Zhang, and M. Ostendorf. 2011. Annotating social acts: Authority claims and alignment moves in wikipedia talk pages. In *Proceedings of ACL – Workshop on Language in Social Media.*

J. S. Bunderson. 2003. Recognizing and utilizing expertise in work groups: A status characteristics perspective. *Administrative Science Quarterly*, 48(4):557–591.

E. Gilbert, T. Bergstrom, and K. Karahalios. 2009. Blogs Are Echo Chambers: Blogs Are Echo Chambers. In *Proceedings of HICSS*, pages 1–10.

T. Hastie, R. Tibshirani, and J. Friedman. 2009. *The Elements of Statistical Learning: Data Mining, Inference, and Prediction, Second Edition.* Springer Series in Statistics. Springer, September.

B. Hutchinson, B. Zhang, and M. Ostendorf. 2010. Unsupervised broadcast conversation speaker role labeling. In *Proceedings of ICASSP*, pages 5322–5325.

S. M. Kim and E. Hovy. 2006. Automatic identification of pro and con reasons in online reviews. In *Proceedings of COLING-ACL*, pages 483–490.

K. Laskowski, M. Ostendorf, and T. Schultz. 2008. Modeling vocal interaction for text-independent participant characterization in multi-party conversation. In *ISCA/ACL SIGdial Workshop on Discourse and Dialogue*, pages 194–201.

F. Liu and Y. Liu. 2007. Soundbite identification using reference and automatic transcripts of broadcast news speech. In *Proceedings of ASRU*, pages 653–658.

Y. Liu. 2006. Initial study on automatic identification of speaker role in broadcast news speech. In *Proceedings of HLT*, pages 81–84.

A. Marin, M. Ostendorf, B. Zhang, J. T. Morgan, M. Oxley, M. Zachry, and E. M. Bender. 2010. Detecting authority bids in online discussions. In *Proceedings of SLT*, pages 49–54.

S. Maskey and J. Hirschberg. 2006. Soundbite detection in broadcast news domain. In *Proceedings of Interspeech*, pages 1543–1546.

A. K. McCallum. 2002. MALLET: A machine learning for language toolkit. http://mallet.cs.umass.edu.

B. Pang and L. Lee. 2004. A Sentimental Education: Sentiment Analysis Using Subjectivity Summarization Based on Minimum Cuts. In *Proceedings of ACL*, pages 271–278.

B. Pang and L. Lee. 2005. Seeing stars: exploiting class relationships for sentiment categorization with respect to rating scales. In *Proceedings of ACL*, pages 115–124.

S. Petrov, L. Barrett, R. Thibaux, and D. Klein. 2006. Learning accurate, compact, and interpretable tree annotation. In *Proceedings of COLING-ACL*, pages 433–440.

A. Vinciarelli. 2007. Speakers role recognition in multiparty audio recordings using social network analysis and duration distribution modeling. *IEEE Transactions on Multimedia*, 9(6):1215–1226.

Y. Yang and J. O. Pedersen. 1997. A Comparative Study on Feature Selection in Text Categorization. In *Proceedings of ICML*, pages 412–420.

Annotating Social Acts: Authority Claims and Alignment Moves in Wikipedia Talk Pages

Emily M. Bender[*], Jonathan T. Morgan[†], Meghan Oxley[*], Mark Zachry[†],
Brian Hutchinson[‡], Alex Marin[‡], Bin Zhang[‡], Mari Ostendorf[‡]
[*]Department of Linguistics, [†]Department of Human Centered Design and Engineering
[‡]Department of Electrical Engineering
University of Washington
{ebender,jmo25,what,zachry}@uw.edu, {brianhutchinson,iskander,binz,mo}@ee.washington.edu

Abstract

We present the AAWD corpus, a collection of 365 discussions drawn from Wikipedia talk pages and annotated with labels capturing two kinds of social acts: alignment moves and authority claims. We describe these social acts and our annotation process, and analyze the resulting data set for interactions between participant status and social acts and between the social acts themselves.

1 Introduction

This paper presents a new annotated resource: the Authority and Alignment in Wikipedia Discussions (AAWD) corpus (available from `http://ssli.ee.washington.edu/projects/SCIL.html`). The AAWD corpus contains discussions from English-language Wikipedia talk pages extracted from the 2008 Wikipedia data dump and annotated for two types of social acts: authority claims and positive/negative alignment moves. In brief, an authority claim is a statement made by a discussion participant aimed at bolstering their credibility in the discussion. An alignment move is a statement by a participant which explicitly positions them as agreeing or disagreeing with another participant or participants regarding a particular topic.

These annotations are intended to make accessible for automated processing two interesting and characteristic aspects of interaction in online discussion forums. As a dataset for computational and sociolinguistic analysis, the discussion pages within Wikipedia are valuable for several reasons. First, the interaction among the participants is nearly entirely captured within the dataset, and all of the "identity-work" (Bucholtz and Hall, 2010) done by Wikipedia discussion participants needs to be done directly in the text of their comments. Furthermore, the discussions tend to be task-driven, focused on the shared goal of improving the associated article. This leads the data to be a particularly rich source of linguistic expressions of authority and alignment.

Our annotations represent a kind of information which is rather different from that involved in NLP tasks such as POS tagging, morphological analysis, parsing and semantic role labeling. Such tasks involve recognizing information that is implicit in the linguistic signal but nonetheless part of its structure. Tasks such as named-entity recognition and word sense disambiguation are also close to the linguistic structure of the signal. Authority claims and alignment moves, on the other hand, are examples of communicative moves aimed at social positioning of a discussant within a group of participants, which may be specialized dialog acts but are referred to here as "social acts." We distinguish social acts from "social events" as described in (Agarwal and Rambow, 2010): social events correspond to types of interactions among people, whereas a social act is associated with a fine-grained social goal and reflected in the specific choices of words and orthographic or prosodic cues at the level of a turn.

The primary value of this new data set is in facilitating computational modeling of a new task type, i.e. the identification of fine-grained social acts in linguistic interaction. While there has been some prior work on detecting agreements and disagreements in multiparty discussions (Hillard et al., 2003; Galley et al., 2004), which is related to detecting positive/negative alignment moves, most previous work on authority bids has involved descriptive studies, e.g. (Galegher et al., 1998). Computational modeling of these phenomena and automatic detection will help with understanding effective argumentation strategies in online discussions and automatic identification of divisive or controversial discussions and online trolls. We believe that these tasks also provide an interesting arena in which to study linguistic feature engineering and feature selection. As with tasks such as sentiment analysis, a simple "bag-of-words" model with word or even n-gram-based features is not sufficiently powerful to detect many instances of these social acts, where combinations of positive and negative words must be interpreted in context, e.g. *absolutely* is positive alone but amplifies a negative in *absolutely not*, and *yeah* in *yeah, I want to correct something John said of course* doesn't necessarily indicate agreement. The typical scenario where hand-annotated training data is limited presents a challenge for learning phrase patterns that discriminate social acts.

In the remainder of this paper, we further describe the social acts and annotation schemata (Section 2), provide details of the AAWD corpus (Section 3), and analyze the distribution of the social acts (Section 4). This analysis describes the distribution of the social acts and tests hypotheses about their interactions with each other and with user status.

2 Annotation Schemata

2.1 Authority Claims

The ability to persuade others to believe in one's statements or the soundness of one's judgments is a necessary component of human social interaction. In order to establish the necessary credibility to secure the belief or assent of others, communicators will often couch their statements in some broadly-recognized basis for authority. These "arguments from authority" have been recognized as an important component of informal logic by many language philosophers (Liu, 1997), including John Locke (1959 [1690]). In recent decades the self-presentation of authority has been studied in a variety of spoken and written contexts by scholars from disciplines such as communication, rhetoric, health studies, sociolinguistics, linguistic pragmatics and political science in order to understand the strategies that communicators operating in different genres and media employ to establish themselves as credible discursive participants. Studies of online product reviews (Mackiewicz, 2010), online political deliberation (Jensen, 2003), scientific publications (Thompson, 1993), online forum posts (Galegher et al., 1998; Richardson, 2003) and radio talk-shows (Thornborrow, 2001) have revealed that considerations of genre, medium and social context all shape the ways interactants attempt to claim the authority to be listened to and taken seriously.

From the perspective of discourse analysis, authority claims provide an interesting lens through which to view a text, as the overall frequency of claims can reflect the nature or purpose of the discourse (e.g. task-oriented collaboration vs. undirected conversation) and the distribution of claim types can reveal features of the social context in which they are made, such as shared norms, practices and community values. For example, since certain bases for authority may be seen as more credible than others in certain contexts (such as citation of peer-reviewed publications in academic scholarship, or references to personal experience in online support groups), the prevalence and distribution of different types of claims in a written text or a conversation transcript can illuminate the shared values of speakers and audiences in a given genre (Galegher et al., 1998). Although the linguistic construction of authority claims can vary greatly according to the genre of the communication, within a single genre there is often great regularity in the ways claims are made, such as the common *I'm a long-time listener* introduction used by radio talk-show call-in guests. Even across genres, recognizable types emerge: references to personal credentials (such as education or profession) are found to be important in newsgroup messages (Richardson, 2003), product reviews (Mackiewicz, 2010) and online scientific article comments (Shanahan, 2010).

Our taxonomy of authority claims was iteratively developed based on our empirical analysis of conversational interaction in two different genres: political talk shows and Wikipedia discussion pages (Oxley et al., 2010), with reference to the literature cited above. Our codebook (available from `http://ssli.ee.washington.edu/projects/SCIL.html`) includes detailed definitions as well as positive and negative examples for each claim type.

We classify authority claims into the following types (examples are drawn from our data):

Credentials: Credentials claims involve reference to education, training, or a history of work in an area. (Ex: *Speaking as a native born Midwesterner who is also a professional writer…*)

Experiential: Experiential claims are based on an individual's involvement in or witnessing of an event. (Ex: *If I recall correctly, God is mentioned in civil ceremonies in Snohomish County, Washington, the only place I've witnessed one.*)

Institutional: Institutional claims are based on an individual's position within an organization structure that governs the current discussion forum or has power to affect the topic or direction of the discussion. (Not attested in our corpus.)

Forum: Forum claims are based on policy, norms, or contextual rules of behavior in the interaction. (Ex: *Do any of these meet wikipedia's [[WP:RS | Reliable Sources]] criteria?*)

External: External claims are based on an outside authority or source of expertise, such as a book, magazine article, website, written law, press release, or court decision. (Ex: *The treaty of international law which states that wars have to begin with a declaration is the Hague Convention relative to the Opening of Hostilities from 1907.*)

Social Expectations: Social Expectations claims are based on the intentions or expectations (what they think, feel or believe) of groups or communities that exist beyond the current conversational context. (Ex: *I think in the minds of most people, including the government, the word "war" and a formal declaration of war have come apart.*)

2.2 Alignment Moves

In multiparty discourse, relationships among participants manifest themselves in social moves that participants make to demonstrate alignment with or against other participants. Expressing alignment with another participant functions as a means of enhancing solidarity with that participant while expressing alignment against another participant maintains social distance between conversational participants, particularly in situations where participants may be previously unacquainted with each other (Svennevig, 1999). Changes in the alignment of participants toward one another or "shifts in footing" may reflect changes in interpersonal relationships or may be more transitory, demonstrating minor concessions and critiques embedded within larger, more stable patterns of participant agreement and disagreement (Goffman, 1981; Wine, 2008).

As Wikipedia editors negotiate about article content, they make statements that support or oppose propositions suggested by other editors and thereby publicly align either with or against other editors in the discussion. Although ways of expressing agreement and disagreement vary according to power relations between participants, participant goals, and conversational context (Rees-Miller, 2000), previous research has suggested that expressions of agreement and disagreement in written language are more explicit than oral expressions of agreement and disagreement (Mulkay, 1985; Mulkay, 1986) and that statements of agreement are particularly explicit in online discussions (Baym, 1996).

We classify alignment moves into positive and negative types, according to whether the participant is agreeing or disagreeing with the target:

Positive alignment moves express agreement with the opinions of another participant. Positive alignment is annotated in cases of explicit agreement, praise/thanking, positive reference to another participant's point (e.g. *As Joe pointed out…*), or where other clear indicators of positive alignment are present.

Negative alignment moves express disagreement with the opinions of another participant. Negative alignment is annotated in cases of explicit disagreement, doubting, sarcastic praise, criticism/insult, dismissing, or where other clear indicators of negative alignment (such as typographical cues) are present.

Based on our experience using the types of authority claims to diagnose and correct sources of inter-annotator disagreement (see §3.3 below), we developed subtypes of positive and negative alignment. While these do not have the same theoretical grounding as the types of authority claims, they did serve the same purpose of improving our annotation over time.

We annotate a target for each alignment move, which may be one or more specific other parties in the conversation, the group as the whole, or someone outside the conversation. In addition, we include a category labeled "unclear" for cases where there is an alignment move, but the annotators are not able to discern its target. Again, the codebook includes example subtypes as part of detailed definitions as well as positive and negative examples for each alignment type.

3 The Corpus

3.1 Source Data

Wikipedia talk pages (also called discussion pages) are editable pages on which editors can take part in threaded, asynchronous discussions about the content of other pages. All editors potentially interested in a given article can join the conversation on that article's talk page. Sometimes these conversations take the form of a deliberative exchange or even a heated argument as editors advocate different ideas about such things as the content or form of an article. Each edit to the talk pages is recorded as a unique revision in the system and thus becomes part of the permanent record of system activity.

Wikipedia constitutes a particularly valuable natural laboratory for studies such as this one, for several reasons. First, the interaction among the participants is almost entirely captured within the Wikipedia database: while some Wikipedians might interact with each other in person or in other online fora (such as IRC or mailing lists), this is the exception rather than the rule. Furthermore, while participants often maintain persistent identities (usernames for registered users; IP addresses for unregistered ones) there are no cues to social identities available to the participants beyond what is captured in the digital record. Therefore all of the effort that participants put into constructing their online identities is in the record for analysis. Second, the discussions on Wikipedia talk pages tend to be goal-oriented, as the discussion topic is the Wikipedia article that the participants are collaboratively editing. This goal-orientation motivates participants to explicitly align with each other in the course of discussions and buttress their arguments with authority claims. Finally, the Wikipedia dataset contains rich metadata, such as the date and time of each edit (identified by revision id) to every article or talk page; the editor responsible for the edit (identified by username or IP address, depending on registration status); and markup such as hyperlinks and formatting used in the textual content of each edit. These metadata allow for sophisticated data analysis at the editor level (e.g. how many edits made by one editor in a given span of time) and the page level (e.g. how many editors have participated in a talk page discussion).

The Wikimedia Foundation frequently releases the database dump of the Wikipedia pages in the form of XML (available at `http://download.wikimedia.org`). The database dumps are categorized into languages, and for each language, there are XML files corresponding to different levels of detail in terms of the information they contain. To get the information on all revisions, we used the largest database dump, which contains all Wikipedia pages and complete edit history. The XML file was parsed and a database created locally with all the revision information for both main pages and talk pages. We then constructed queries to retrieve the main pages and corresponding talk pages based on a list of topics for which extensive discussions are likely to occur.

Our data is drawn from a set of 365 discussions from 47 talk pages. The discussions were selected to contain at least 5 turns and at least 4 human participants.[1] The earliest edit in our data set is from January 29, 2002 and the latest is from January 6, 2008. A total of 1,509 editors collectively make 6,066 turns in this data. Of the 365 discussions, 185 were annotated for both alignment moves and authority claims. An additional 26 were annotated for alignment only and an additional 154 were annotated for authority only. The numbers of editors and turns in these sets are shown in Table 1.

3.2 Annotation Units

A Wikipedia talk page is in itself a wiki-style document. Thus, each modification to a talk page by an editor can modify multiple sections of the page. We define a "turn" as a contiguous body of text on the

[1]Wikipedia discussions may also include contributions by automated "bots".

	Annotated for		
	authority	alignment	both
pages	47	36	36
discussions	339	211	185
editors	1,417	988	896
turns	5,636	3,390	2,960

Table 1: Pages, discussions, editors and turns in annotated data

corresponding page that was modified as part of a single revision. Thus, a single revision may result in multiple turns being added. Each turn may include one or more paragraphs of text, either existing but modified, or new additions. We annotated authority claims at the paragraph level and alignment moves at the turn level. The larger unit is used for alignment moves because the phenomenon as defined can span a larger section of text.

The annotation tool (a modified version of LDC's XTrans (Glenn et al., 2009)) allowed annotators to indicate the presence and type of claims or moves in each annotation unit, in addition to selecting spans of text corresponding to each social act. For alignment moves, within a turn, alignment of the same type (positive or negative) with the same target was annotated as a single alignment move, even across multiple sentences. Where the type or target differed, we annotated up to three separate alignment moves per annotation unit. For authority claims, we also annotated up to three claims per annotation unit, with each claim identified by a single span of text. Claims in separate sentences of an annotation unit counted as separate even if they were of the same type. Figure 1 gives an example from our codebook of a turn with multiple alignment moves.

3.3 Annotation Process

Each discussion thread was annotated independently by two or more annotators. Inter-annotator agreement was calculated at weekly intervals to assess annotation progress and identify areas of disagreement. Adjudicators also performed "spot checks" of annotated data weekly and provided feedback when there were disagreements among annotators or when codes seemed to be inconsistently or erroneously applied. The codebooks for authority claims and alignment moves were also iteratively refined with the addition of positive and negative examples and specific linguistic cues commonly associated with particular move or claim types based on spot-check results and annotator feedback.

Two strategies that proved useful in maintaining consistency in the frequency and reliability of coding across annotators were the computation of average agreement and comparison of overall counts of each codable unit on a weekly basis. Computing average agreement allowed adjudicators to identify particular categories that were proving especially difficult to code consistently, and to better focus their efforts on re-training annotators and updating the relevant sections of the annotation guidelines. Comparing counts of the number of times two annotators had coded a particular category over the same number of discussions also proved useful for identifying potential problems with under- or over-coding of a category by a particular annotator.

3.4 Reconciliation

The manual annotation process was completed independently by each annotator, resulting in multiple sets of labels. To create a single copy of the data that can be used in learning experiments, an algorithm was designed to merge the annotations into a single, "master" version. The algorithm balances annotation consistency and simplicity of the merging process. We treat the annotations for each unit in a file as a set with respect to type: Multiple labels of the same type are treated as a single label for purposes of reconciliation, with only one label of each type allowed for each annotation unit.

We mark each social act which had been identified by at least two annotators as having "high confidence." If a social act was identified by only one annotator in that annotation unit, it is marked as having "low confidence." This procedure yields two sets of social act types found in each annotation unit, one consisting of the high confidence labels, and another of the low confidence labels. The labels from each set are kept distinct, i.e. for each label in the high confidence set, the corresponding label in the low confidence set has the suffix "_single" appended to the high confidence label.

Aggregated social act labels are propagated to the sentence level by using a dynamic programming algorithm to match sentences (determined by automatic segmentation) with the keyword spans

speaker	turn	transcript	alignment1	alignment2	alignment3
S1	3	<k1>S2, I think you're right</k1>. <k2>S3's idea is way off base </k2>, but <k1> you seem to have a good solution</k1>. <k3>But I disagree with your name for the section</k3> — Iraq War is used in the United States media and should be used here as well.	positive:S2::explicit_agreement	negative:S3::explicit_disagreement	negative:S2::explicit_disagreement

Figure 1: Example from alignment codebook

based on overlap. A sentence could have multiple positive labels if one or more annotators labeled it for different types in the high or low confidence set. Sentences in turns with a marked social act but not aligned to text spans are labeled as "unused" due to the ambiguity associated with a limit on the number of social acts annotated per unit. All sentences in an annotation unit for which no annotator found any positive labels are labeled with the negative class. The data distributed at http://ssli.ee.washington.edu/projects/SCIL.html include both the underlying per-annotator files as well as the files output by the reconciliation process.

3.5 Annotation Quality

In complicated annotation tasks, such as those conducted in this work, establishing reliable ground truth is a fundamental challenge. The most popular approach to measuring annotation quality is via the surrogate of annotation consistency. This assumes that when annotators working independently arrive at the same decisions they have correctly carried out the task specified by the annotation guidelines. Several quantitative measures of annotator consistency have been proposed and debated over the years (Artstein and Poesio, 2008). We use the well-known Cohen's kappa coefficient κ, which accounts for uneven class priors, so one may obtain a low agreement score even when a high percentage of tokens have the same label. We also report the percentage of instances on which the annotators agreed, A, which includes agreement on the absence of a particular label. When a set of instances have been labeled by more than two annotators, we compute the average of pairwise agreement.

Scores for authority claim and alignment move agreement are presented in Tables 2 and 3.[2] For authority, the most common types of claims, forum and external, are also two of the most reliably identified. For alignment, the positive type has much better agreement scores than the negative type. Interestingly, it appears that the fine distinctions between the types of negative alignment move are a large factor in the low agreement scores. When all of the negative categories are merged, agreement is higher, although still less than for positive alignment moves.

Our κ values generally fall within the range that Landis and Koch (1977) deem "moderate agreement", but below the .8 cut-off tentatively suggested

Claim Type	N	κ	A
forum	451	0.52	0.92
external	715	0.63	0.91
experiential	185	0.33	0.96
social expectations	78	0.13	0.98
credentials	6	0.57	0.99
Overall	1157	0.59	0.86

Table 2: Agreement summary for authority claims. N denotes the number of turns of the given type that at least one annotator marked.

Move Type	N	κ	A
explicit agreement	379	0.62	0.94
praise/thanking	117	0.60	0.98
positive reference	86	0.20	0.98
explicit disagreement	453	0.29	0.92
doubting	198	0.23	0.96
sarcastic praise	38	0.30	0.99
criticism/insult	556	0.32	0.91
dismissing	396	0.16	0.91
All positive	509	0.66	0.94
All negative	1092	0.45	0.85
Overall	1378	0.50	0.80

Table 3: Agreement summary for alignment moves. N denotes the number of turns of the given type that at least one annotator marked.

[2] Institutional claims are exceedingly rare in our data, appearing in only three labels. This is not sufficient for proper κ computation, and so we do not include them in Table 3.

by Artstein and Poesio (2008).[3] One possible reason is that the negative class is not as discrete as it might be in other tasks: both alignment moves and authority claims can be more or less subtle or explicit. We have designed our annotation guidelines to emphasize the more explicit variants of each, but the same guidelines can sometimes lead annotators to pick up more subtle examples that other annotators might not feel meet the strict definitions in the guidelines. Thus we expect our "high-confidence" labels to correspond to the more blatant examples and the "low-confidence" labels, while sometimes being genuine noise, to pick out more subtle examples.

4 Analysis

While the main goal of this paper is to document the AAWD corpus, we also performed several statistical analyses of authority and alignment, in order to demonstrate the relevance of these social acts as markers of user identity and social dynamics within our corpus. In this section we present the overall distribution of authority claims and alignment moves, compare the prevalence of authority claims across user types, and show how a participant's claim-making behavior may affect how others subsequently align with them. In doing so, we consider only high-confidence labels from files which were annotated by at least two annotators. This subset includes 186 discussions annotated for alignment moves and 200 discussions annotated for authority claims. Of those, 149 discussions were annotated for both types of social acts.

4.1 Distribution of Social Acts

We find that 25% of the turns in our alignment data contain alignment moves and 21% of the turns in our authority data contain authority claims. In addition, 35% and 32% of the editors in each set make alignment moves and authority claims, respectively. The breakdown by alignment move and authority claim type is given in Table 4. Note that any given turn might contain both positive and negative alignment moves or multiple types of authority claims.

[3] Artstein and Poesio also note that it may not make sense to have only one threshold for the field.

	N	%
Alignment data		
total turns	2,890	100
turns w/positive alignment	330	11.4
turns w/negative alignment	467	16.2
turns w/any alignment	710	24.6
total editors	905	100
editors w/alignment moves	315	34.8
Authority data		
total turns	3,361	100
turns w/external claim	459	13.7
turns w/forum claim	260	7.7
turns w/experiential claim	77	2.3
turns w/soc. exp. claim	21	0.6
turns w/credentials claim	3	0.1
turns w/institutional claim	0	0
turns w/any claim	703	20.9
total editors	930	100
editors w/authority claims	297	31.9

Table 4: Summary of high-confidence alignment moves and authority claims

4.2 Authority Claim Types by User Status

Wikipedia distinguishes three different statuses: unregistered users (able to perform most editing activities, identified only by IP address), registered users (able to perform more editing activities, edits attributed to a consistent user name) and administrators (registered users with additional 'sysop' privileges). Participants of different statuses tend to do different kinds of work on Wikipedia, with administrators in particular being more likely to take on moderator work (Burke and Kraut, 2008), such as mediating and diffusing disputes among editors. Because conflict mediation requires a different kind of credibility than collaborative writing work, and because unregistered users are likely to be newer and therefore less likely to be incorporating references to Wikipedia-specific rules and norms into their projected identities (and, therefore, their conversation), we hypothesized that editors of different statuses would use different kinds of authority claims.

Indeed, this is borne out. While no user group was significantly more or less likely than any other to include authority claims overall in their posts (chi square test for independence, n=3164, df=2, χ^2=2.367, p=.306) users of different statuses did use significantly different proportions of each type of claim (chi square test for independence, n=973, df=8

Participant type	# users	% forum	% external	% claim-bearing turns
admin	44	47.1	45.1	19.6
reg	192	29.1	63.6	22.3
unreg	55	18.3	70.6	19.8
all	291	29.8	62.5	21.6

Table 5: Percentage of authority claims of forum and external types, and percentage of total turns which contained claims, across user statuses

χ^2=38.301, p<.001). As illustrated in Table 5, administrators are more likely than the other groups to make forum claims and less likely to make external claims, unregistered users make more external claims and fewer forum claims, and registered users exhibit a claim distribution that more closely reflects the overall distribution of claim types.

4.3 Authority Claim Prevalence by V-Index

Given the few visible markers of status on Wikipedia and the fact that editors are constantly interacting with new collaborators, Wikipedians perform authority by adopting insider language and norms of interaction. Supporting arguments with specific references is one such norm. Thus we hypothesized that as editors become more integrated into Wikipedia, they will make more authority claims. In order to test this hypothesis, we developed "v-index" as a proxy measure of degree of integration or "veteran status" within the community. Inspired by Ball's (2005) "h-index" of scholarly productivity, v-index balances frequency of interaction with length of interaction. Specifically, an editor's v-index at the time of a particular revision is the greatest v such that the editor has made at least v edits within the past v months (28-day periods).

We measured the v-index for each revision in our dataset, using all edits to Wikipedia in order to calculate v (not just edits to the discussions we have annotated). The v-index values for edits within our dataset range from 1 to 46.[4] We measured the proportion of turns with authority claims (of any type) for each v-index. The proportion of turns with authority claims is in fact positively correlated with v-index, confirming our hypothesis (one-sided Pearson's correlation coefficient, n=29 v-indices, r=0.371, p=0.024).

[4]The data becomes very sparse for v-indices above 29, with every v-index in this range represented by < 10 turns, so the v-indices of 30-46 were not included in this analysis.

Initial turn	Alignment in next 10 turns
no auth. claim	0.52
any auth. claim	0.63

Table 6: Average prevalence of alignment moves targeted at participant in 10 following turns

4.4 Interaction of Social Phenomena

Thus far, we have been addressing our social acts independently, but of course no social act occurs in a vacuum. Alignment moves and authority claims are only two types of social acts; many other types of social acts are present (and could be annotated) in this same data set. Even with only these two types (and their subtypes), however, we find interactions.

We hypothesized that authority claims would be likely to provoke alignment moves. That is, although participants may make alignment moves whenever someone else has expressed an opinion or taken action (e.g. edited the article attached to the discussion), we hypothesized that by making an authority claim, a participant becomes more likely to become a focal point in the debate. To test this, we calculated, for every turn, the number of alignment moves targeted at the author of that turn within the next 10 turns. We then divided the turns into those that contained authority claims and those that did not. Making an authority claim in a given turn made the participant significantly more likely to be the target of an alignment move within the subsequent 10 turns compared to turns that did not contain any claims (t=-2.086, df=772, p=.037; Table 6))

Furthermore, we find that different types of authority claims elicit different numbers of subsequent alignment moves. Specifically, turns that contain either external claims or forum claims (the two most prevalent claim types in our sample) interact differently with alignment. External claims elicited more alignment overall (t=3.189, df=411, p=.002) and more negative alignment moves than did forum claims (t=3.839, df=415, p<.001). However, external claims did not elicit significantly more positive alignment moves than forum claims (t=0.695, df=309, p=.488). This is illustrated in Table 7.

Initial turn	Alignment in next 10 turns		
	positive	negative	overall
external claim	0.26	0.49	0.74
forum claim	0.22	0.20	0.42

Table 7: Average prevalence of alignment moves targeted at participant in 10 following turns

5 Conclusion

We have presented the Authority and Alignment in Wikipedia Discussions (AAWD) corpus, a collection of 365 discussions drawn from Wikipedia talk pages and annotated for two broad types of social acts: authority claims and alignment moves. These annotations make explicit important discursive strategies that discussion participants use to construct their identities in this online forum. That "identity work" is being done with these social acts is confirmed by the correlations we find between proportions of turns with authority claims and external variables such as user status and v-index, on the one hand, and the interaction between authority claims and alignment moves on the other.

As an example of a social medium, Wikipedia is characterized by its task-orientation and by the fact that all of the interactants' "identity work" with respect to their identity in the medium is captured in the database. This, in turn, causes the data set to be rich in the type of social acts we are investigating. The dataset was used for research in automatic detection of forum claims, as presented in a companion paper (Marin et al., 2011). That work focused on using lexical features, filtered through word lists obtained from domain experts and through data-driven methods, and extended with parse tree information. Automatic detection of other types of authority claims and of alignment moves is left for future research.

We believe that, as social acts, authority claims and alignment moves are broadly recognized communication behaviors that play an important role in human interaction across a variety of contexts. However, because Wikipedia discussions are shaped by a set of well-defined, local communication norms which are closely tied to the task of distributed, collaborative writing, we expect authority claims and alignment moves will manifest differently in other genres. Future work could explore the range of variation among the linguistic cues associated with authority and alignment categories across genres, cultures and communication media, as well as the possible role of additional categories or social acts not discussed here. We believe that the communicative ecology of Wikipedia discussions, combined with the rich metadata of the Wikipedia database, presents a highly valuable natural laboratory in which to explore social scientific analyses of communication behaviors as well as a resource for the development of NLP systems which can automatically identify these social acts, in Wikipedia and beyond.

Acknowledgments

This research was funded by the Office of the Director of National Intelligence (ODNI), Intelligence Advanced Research Projects Activity (IARPA). All statements of fact, opinion or conclusions contained herein are those of the authors and should not be construed as representing the official views or policies of IARPA, the ODNI or the U.S. Government.

The original Wikipedia discussion page data for this study was made available from a research project supported by NSF award IIS-0811210. We thank Travis Kriplean for his initial assistance with scripts to process this data dump.

We also gratefully acknowledge the contribution of the annotators: Wendy Kempsell, Kelley Kilanski, Robert Sykes and Lisa Tittle.

References

Apoorv Agarwal and Owen Rambow. 2010. Automatic detection and classification of social events. In *Proceedings of the 2010 Conference on Empirical Methods in Natural Language Processing*, pages 1024–1034, Cambridge, MA. Association for Computational Linguistics.

Ron Artstein and Massimo Poesio. 2008. Inter-coder agreement for computational linguistics. *Computational Linguistics*, 34(4):555–596.

Philip Ball. 2005. Index aims for fair ranking of scientists. *Nature*, 436:900–900.

Nancy Baym. 1996. Agreements and disagreements in a computer-mediated discussion. *Research on Language and Social Interaction*, 29:315–345.

Mary Bucholtz and Kira Hall. 2010. Locating identity in language. In C. Llamas and D. Watt, editors, *Lan-*

guage and Identities. Edinburgh University Press, Edinburgh.

Moira Burke and Robert Kraut. 2008. Mopping up: Modeling wikipedia promotion decisions. In *Proceedings of the 2008 ACM Conference on Computer Supported Cooperative Work*, pages 27–36. Association of Computing Machinery.

Jolene Galegher, Lee Sproull, and Sara Kiesler. 1998. Legitimacy, authority, and community in electronic support groups. *Written Communication*, 15(4):493–530.

Michel Galley, Kathleen McKeown, Julia Hirschberg, and Elizabeth Shriberg. 2004. Identifying agreement and disagreement in conversational speech: Use of Bayesian networks to model pragmatic dependencies. In *Proceedings of the 42nd Meeting of the Association for Computational Linguistics (ACL'04), Main Volume*, pages 669–676, Barcelona, Spain.

Meghan Lammie Glenn, Stephanie M. Strassel, and Haejoong Lee. 2009. XTrans: A speech annotation and transcription tool. In *INTERSPEECH-2009*, pages 2855–2858.

Erving Goffman. 1981. *Forms of Talk*. University of Pennsylvania Press, Philadelphia.

Dustin Hillard, Mari Ostendorf, and Elizabeth Shriberg. 2003. Detection of agreement vs. disagreement in meetings: training with unlabeled data. In *Proceedings of the 2003 Human Language Technology Conference of the North American Chapter of the Association for Computational Linguistics (HLT/NAACL)*, pages 34–36.

Jakob L. Jensen. 2003. Public spheres on the internet: Anarchic or government sponsored; a comparison. *Scandinavian Political Studies*, 26:349–374.

J. Richard Landis and Gary G. Koch. 1977. Measurement of observer agreement for categorical data. *Biometrics*, 33:159–174.

Yameng Liu. 1997. Authority, presumption and invention. *Philosophy and Rhetoric*, 30(4):413–427.

John Locke. 1959 [1690]. *An Essay Concerning Human Understanding*. Dover Publications, New York.

Jo Mackiewicz. 2010. Assertions of expertise in online product reviews. *Journal of Business and Technical Communication*, 24(1):3–28.

Alex Marin, Bin Zhang, and Mari Ostendorf. 2011. Detecting forum authority claims in online discussions. *Proceedings of the Workshop on Language in Social Media (LSM 2011)*.

Michael Mulkay. 1985. Agreement and disagreement in conversations and letters. *Text*, 5(3):201–227.

Michael Mulkay. 1986. Conversations and texts. *Human Studies*, 9(2-3):303–321.

Meghan Oxley, Jonathan T. Morgan, Mark Zachry, and Brian Hutchinson. 2010. "What I know is...": Establishing credibility on Wikipedia talk pages. In *Proceedings of the 6th International Symposium on Wikis and Open Collaboration*, Gdansk, Poland. Association for Computing Machinery.

Janie Rees-Miller. 2000. Power, severity, and context in disagreeement. *Journal of Pragmatics*, 32(8):1087–1111.

Kay Richardson. 2003. Health risks on the internet: Establishing credibility on line. *Health, Risk and Society*, 5(2):171–184.

Marie-Claire Shanahan. 2010. Changing the meaning of peer-to-peer? Exploring online comment spaces as sites of negotiated expertise. *Journal of Science Communication*, 9(1):1–13.

Jan Svennevig. 1999. *Getting Acquainted in Conversation: A Study of Initial Interactions*. John Benjamins Publishing Company, Amsterdam.

Dorothea K. Thompson. 1993. Arguing for experimental "facts" in science. *Written Communication*, 10:106.

Joanna Thornborrow. 2001. Authenticating talk: Building public identities in audience participation broadcasting. *Discourse Studies*, 3(4):459–479.

Linda Wine. 2008. Towards a deeper understanding of framing, footing, and alignment. *Teachers College, Columbia University Working Papers in TESOL and Applied Linguistics*, 8(3):1–3.

Analyzing the Dynamic Evolution of Hashtags on Twitter: a Language-Based Approach

Evandro Cunha[1] **Gabriel Magno**[1] **Giovanni Comarela**[1]
Virgilio Almeida[1] **Marcos André Gonçalves**[1] **Fabrício Benevenuto**[2]
[1]Computer Science Department, Federal University of Minas Gerais (UFMG), Brazil
[2]Computer Science Department, Federal University of Ouro Preto (UFOP), Brazil
{evandrocunha, magno, giovannicomarela, virgilio, mgoncalv, fabricio}@dcc.ufmg.br

Abstract

Hashtags are used in Twitter to classify messages, propagate ideas and also to promote specific topics and people. In this paper, we present a linguistic-inspired study of how these tags are created, used and disseminated by the members of information networks. We study the propagation of hashtags in Twitter grounded on models for the analysis of the spread of linguistic innovations in speech communities, that is, in groups of people whose members linguistically influence each other. Differently from traditional linguistic studies, though, we consider the evolution of terms in a live and rapidly evolving stream of content, which can be analyzed in its entirety. In our experimental results, using a large collection crawled from Twitter, we were able to identify some interesting aspects – similar to those found in studies of (offline) speech – that led us to believe that hashtags may effectively serve as models for characterizing the propagation of linguistic forms, including: (1) the existence of a "preferential attachment process", that makes the few most common terms ever more popular, and (2) the relationship between the length of a tag and its frequency of use. The understanding of formation patterns of successful hashtags in Twitter can be useful to increase the effectiveness of real-time streaming search algorithms.

1 Introduction

The use of hashtags is a way to categorize messages posted on Twitter, an important social networking and microblogging service with 175 million registered users (Twitter, 2010), according to the topic of the message. They can be used not only to add context and metadata to the posts, but also for promotion and publicity. By simply adding a hash symbol (#) before a string of letters, numerical digits or underscore signs (_), it is possible to tag a message, helping other users to find tweets that have a common topic. Hashtags allow users to create communities of people interested in the same topic by making it easier for them to find and share information related to it (Kricfalusi, 2009). Figure 1 shows an example of query for the tag "#basketball", which returns the newest tweets with this hashtag.

Figure 1. Example of query for a hashtag on Twitter. Hashtags are not case-sensitive, thus "#basketball" also returns "#Basketball", for example. Tweets with the term "basketball" (without the hash symbol) do not appear in a search for hashtags.

As hashtags are created by the users themselves, a new social event can lead to the simultaneous emergence of several different tags, each one generated by a different user. They can either be accepted by other members of the network or not. In this manner, some propagate and thrive, while others die immediately after birth and are restricted to a few messages.

Similarly, lexical innovations occur when new terms are added to the lexicon of a language, either through the creation of new words, the reuse of existing words or the loan from other languages, for example. An innovation tends to come from one speaker, who proposes it to other members of his speech community – i.e., to whom he is connected in a network of linguistic contacts and influences. Afterwards, these speakers make a cultural selection of the innovation, accepting it or rejecting it.

In the context of the network theory, Figure 2 indicates two moments of a novelty's propagation process: the precise time of the innovation (left) and a later point (right), when some individuals have accepted the innovation, while others, although possibly knowing it, didn't. An innovative linguistic form can get, for some reason, some prestige, and maybe speakers begin to use it, taking it under certain circumstances and transforming it into a variation of the previously hegemonic form.

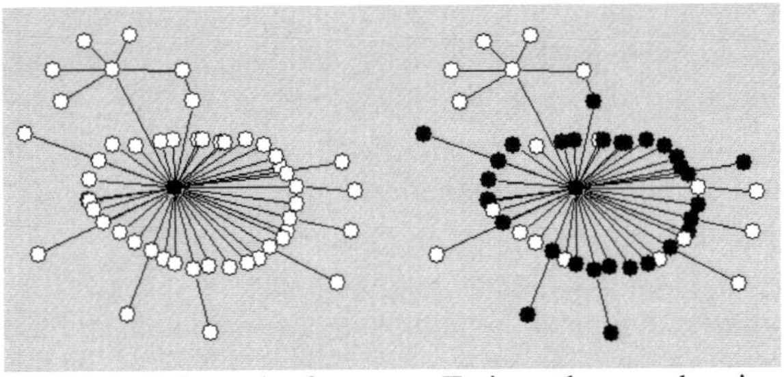

Figure 2. Subgraphs from our Twitter dataset showing two distinct moments in the process of spreading an innovation. The black nodes indicate individuals who joined the innovation (in this case, the hashtag #musicmonday) at a given moment; the white ones indicate individuals who didn't. The links represent follower relationship.

The diffusion of innovations, be they linguistic, behavioral, technological, etc., occurs through a cascade in which the network members, consciously or not, make choices, taking into account a number of factors that determine which forms, behaviors or technologies are more advantageous to be adopted in a given moment (Easley and Kleinberg, 2010).

An important question in the field of linguistics is: how can an initially rare variant spread to an entire linguistic network, or speech community (Sapir, 1921)? How does the linguistic change take out (Silva, 2006)? This change, consisting in the dissemination of less common variants to much of the network or even across the entire network, can be seen as an unexpected fact. However, it occurs. Thus, to better understand the phenomenon of language change, it seems essential to understand the propagation behavior of innovative forms. Understanding how these forms spread – how and where they are born, who are the major disseminators, which network features allow greater dissemination – is the main objective of our research group.

In this work, we examine aspects of the dissemination of hashtags in Twitter, aiming at understanding the process of propagation of innovative hashtags in light of linguistic theories. The utilization of an online social network's dataset allows the review of a linguistic system in its entirety, thereby eliminating the need to work with sampling. It also allows the verification of temporal propagation, enabling a more precise understanding of the path followed by innovations in the network.

Here, we seek to answer mostly two questions: (1) does the distribution of the hashtags in frequency rankings follow some pattern, as the words in the lexicon of a language? (2) Is the length of a hashtag a factor that influences to its success or failure? Our assumption is that identifying linguistic features related to the creation and usage of hashtags in Twitter may raise awareness about individuals' tagging behavior over networks, which is an interesting topic in the field of Network Sciences, Sociology and Social Psychology. Beyond that, this kind of analysis should be interesting to optimize tag recommendation systems not only on Twitter, but on many other online environments, and to increase the effectiveness of real-time streaming search algorithms.

In the next section, we will discuss related works in Linguistics and in Computer Science. We try to always keep contact with linguistic theories, as we believe that complex issues, involving many aspects together, can be better analyzed through a multidisciplinary approach. The following sections cover discussions and the empirical research that was conducted during this study.

2 Related work

Much has been written about linguistic innovations, language variation and language change since Weinreich et al. (1968), which is considered one of the ground works for sociolinguistics. More recently, Troutman et al. (2008) conducted a study with the purpose of simulating language change in a speech community. They built a computational model based on characteristics from language users and from social network structures and tested it in different scenarios, obtaining a probabilistic model that captures many of the key features of language change. Our work extends the traditional way of conducting research on sociolinguistics as we used a corpus of non-natural language data and even so we found compatible results to the ones obtained from natural language data.

Kwak et al. (2010) were the first to study in a quantitative way the topological characteristics of Twitter, information diffusion on it and its power as a new medium of information sharing. Their analyses are in some way related to the ones we perform here. Chew and Eysenbach (2010) led a study that investigated the keywords "swine flu" and "H1N1" on Twitter during the 2009 H1N1 pandemic. The goals of this work were to monitor the use of these terms over time, to conduct a content analysis of tweets and to validate Twitter as a trend-tracking tool. They found the existence of variability in the use of the terms, which is a constitutive aspect of human language. Our findings complement, with more focus on the linguistic approach, what they have discovered, revealing new aspects that can link the creation of hashtags to linguistic innovations.

Romero et al. (2011) studied the mechanics of information diffusion on Twitter. They analyzed the phenomenon of the spread of hashtags, but focusing on the variations of the diffusion features across different topics. Their work introduces the measures "stickiness" – the probability of adoption of one hashtag based on the number of exposures – and "persistence" – which captures how rapidly the influence curve decays. We analyze hashtags as well, but in a different perspective, concentrating on the characteristics that they may have in common with natural language.

3 Dataset and methodology

In our study, we use a dataset consisting of about 2 billion follow links among almost 55 million users. Twitter allowed the collection of data for each existing user, including their social connections, and all the tweets they ever posted. Out of all users, about 8% of the profiles were set private by the users themselves, and only authorized followers could view their tweets. We ignore these users in our analysis. In total, we analyzed more than 1.7 billion tweets posted between July 2006 and August 2009. For a comprehensive description of the data collected we refer the reader to Cha et al. (2010).

As, in some of our analysis, we intend to compare features of the variation of hashtags to linguistic variation, we must find interchangeable hashtags, i.e., different tags used with the same purpose, to characterize messages on the same topic. This corresponds to the basic feature of variant linguistic forms, which are used by different speakers, or at different moments, to name the same object, action etc. Aiming to find interchangeable hashtags, we collected tweets on specific topics. In this way, we could verify the existence of different hashtags used to categorize messages that could be grouped into one category. For example, hashtags like #michaeljackson #mj, #jackson, among many others, refer to the same subject and in a managed environment they would probably be condensed under only one tag.

We selected three relevant topics of this period, namely: Michael Jackson (the singer's death has been widely reported in the social networks), Swine Flu (the epidemic of H1N1 was a major issue of 2009), and Music Monday (this topic is related to a very successful campaign in favor of posting tweets related to music on Mondays). Then, we built one minor base for each one of the topics: MJ (referring to Michael Jackson), SF (referring to Swine Flu) and MM (referring to Music Monday). These bases were formed by filtering tweets that: (1) included at least one hashtag and (2) included at least one of the following terms that we considered related to the topics: "michael jackson" (for the base MJ), "swine flu" or "#swineflu" (for the base SF), and "#musicmonday" (for the base MM). Consequently, in the base MJ, for example, we gathered all the tweets that included the term "michael jackson" and that had at least one hashtag, even if this tag had no direct relationship with the topic.

Table 1 presents data from each base: number of tweets posted, number of users who posted tweets, number of follow links among users of the base and number of different hashtags used in the tweets of the base.

Base	Tweets	Users	Follow links	Different hashtags
MJ	221,128	91,176	3,171,118	19,679
SF	295,333	83,211	5,806,407	17,196
MM	835,883	196,411	7,136,213	16,005

Table 1. Summary information about the bases built.

4 Comparing Twitter to a natural linguistic system

The directionality of both networks we are studying, i.e. Twitter and speech communities, in addition to the resemblance between the creation of hashtags and linguistic innovations, is an important similarity between these systems. It led to the hypothesis that these structures would have more issues in common.

In this section, we discuss these qualitative similarities, in order to justify the following quantitative comparisons.

4.1 Hashtags and linguistic innovations

A linguistic innovation can be described as any change in any existing language system (Breivik and Jahr, 1989). In linguistics, to say that there was an innovation means that there was a modification, a transformation, in any part of the language – phonetics, phonology, syntax, semantics etc. This novelty is neither degeneration, nor an improvement: language changes and evolves, as a living being, in order to adapt itself to the society in which it is inserted.

We use linguistic knowledge to analyze and explain phenomena related to the creation, usage and dissemination of hashtags. We see similarities between these two systems: like linguistic innovations, new hashtags are created by individuals when they feel the need to categorize their messages with a term not yet used for this purpose. This reflects the speaker's need to create a term, for example, to name an object or an action that he/she was not acquainted with in the offline world.

Just like hashtags can fail and be used only once, a linguistic innovation may not exceed the boundaries of its creator's language. An innovation can be used in a specific situation and fall into oblivion, like many linguistic forms which are lost without even being recorded.

4.2 Directionality of the graphs

Twitter's network can be described as a directed graph. On this social network, relations between users are not necessarily symmetrical, which means that it is possible for someone to follow another person without being followed by him/her. This is very clear when we talk about celebrities who have millions of followers, but at the same time follow only a few users.

This characteristic corresponds to the general absence of directionality of offline social networks. Not only on Twitter the edges can go one-way: in the "real world", we are somehow connected to celebrities, athletes and famous politicians, and we hear what they say. We are all part of the same speech community, in the sense that a celebrity is able to influence the way we use language. However, they certainly do not even know who we are: it is like on Twitter's graph, where we follow them, but they do not follow us.

5 Rich-get-richer phenomenon and Zipf's law

Easley and Kleinberg (2010) characterize what is known as "rich-get-richer phenomenon" or "preferential attachment process": in some systems, the popularity of the most common items tends to increase faster than the popularity of the less common ones. It generates a further spread of the forms that achieve a certain prestige.

Zipf (1949) examined and confirmed that the frequency of words in English and in other languages follow a power law. Aiming to verify if any kind of pattern is followed in the tags distribution, we analyzed our data from Twitter.

Tables 2 and 3 display information on the distribution of hashtags in each of the bases studied. By "*i*-tweet hashtags", we mean the hashtags that appear in at most *i* tweets. They are the less common ones. By "*j*-tweet hashtags", we mean the hashtags that appear in at least *j* tweets, that is, the most popular ones.

Base	% of *i*-tweet hashtags inside the base		
	***i*=1**	***i*=2**	***i*=10**
MJ	59%	72%	88%
SF	59%	73%	92%
MM	60%	74%	91%

Table 2. Distribution of less common hashtags of each base.

Base	number of *j*-tweet hashtags inside the base		
	***j*=10,000**	***j*=5,000**	***j*=1,000**
MJ	3	6	28
SF	3	4	14
MM	2	3	28

Table 3. Distribution of most popular hashtags of each base.

The percentage of hashtags according to the number of tweets in which they appear are remarkably very similar in the three bases. It seems to confirm the possible existence of a "rich-get-richer" pattern: few hashtags – the most popular ones – are used in most of the tweets, while the vast majority of them are used in only a few posts. Table 2 shows that around 60% of hashtags are used only once in tweets of the respective base, i.e. do not propagate to the rest of the network; around 90% of them are not used more than ten times, which shows that the great part of the hashtags get restricted to only one user or to a very small community of users.

On the other hand, just like Zipf (1949) showed for natural languages, the most used hashtags get very high frequencies of use. Table 4 shows data from the three most used hashtags in each of the bases and makes clear that, also on Twitter, a person´s behavior depends on the choices made by other people (Easley and Kleinberg, 2010).

Complementing these data, Figure 3 associates the position of a hashtag in a popularity ranking (based on the number of times that a hashtag has been used) to the volume of tweets in which it appears. A plot in log-log coordinates, where x is a rank of a tag in the frequency table and y is the total number of the tag's occurrences in tweets, shows that the distribution of hashtags on Twitter also follow the general trend of a Zipfian distribuction, appearing approximately linear on log-log plot.

Base	Most used	2nd most used	3rd most used
MJ	#michaeljackson 35,861 12.3%	#michael 27,298 9.3%	#mj 16,758 5.7%
SF	#swineflu 230,457 51.5%	#h1n1 70,693 15.8%	#swine 12,444 2.8%
MM	#musicmonday 824,778 79.7%	#musicmondays 11,770 1.1%	#music 5,106 0.5%

Table 4. Data from the most used hashtags of each base. Below each hashtag are given the number of times it was used and the percentage that it represents of the total use of hashtags in the base.

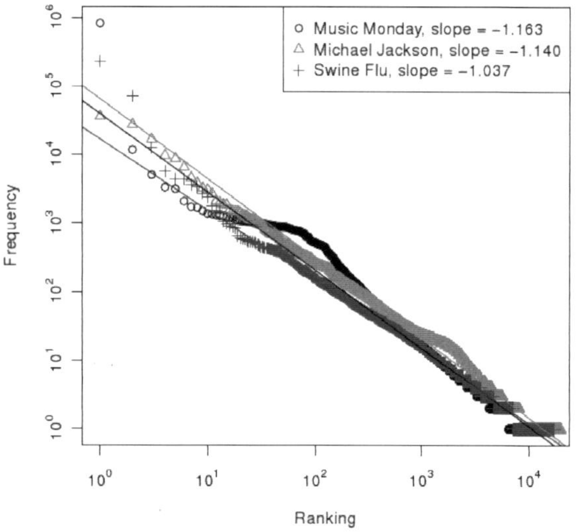

Figure 3. A log-log plot showing volume of tweets in which the hashtag was used vs. its position in a popularity ranking.

Only three values on the left, which refer to tags that occupy the top positions in the frequency ranking (and thus were used more often), are not well described by the interpolations: the most frequent tag on MM base and the two most frequent ones on SF base. This is due to the very high usage of these hashtags: #musicmonday appeared in almost 830,000 tweets of its base; #swineflu, in more than 230,000; and #h1n1, in more than 70,000. The other values, however, show that this is a very good fitting model for our purposes.

It is interesting to notice the similarity of results despite being completely different topics. Even the slopes of the interpolation curves are similar, varying from -1.037 to -1.163.

6 Hashtag length and frequency

Each word or phrase spoken by someone tells a story and reflects characteristics of this individual and his/her group. According to the Theory of Language Variation and Change (Weinreich et al., 1968; Labov, 1995, 2001), lexical choice is the result of a series of social interactions that make up and form, little by little, the individual speech. Naturally, these interactions and influences are so subtle that we ourselves hardly realize them: gender, age, location, social role, hierarchical position in an organization – all this reflects the way we use language in various situations of everyday life. Understanding what makes speakers choose one of the forms in variation, in certain situations, is one of the goals of Sociolinguistics.

In addition to these social factors that influence the way we express ourselves, described by Labov (2001), there are also many strictly linguistic factors which perform such influence, as Labov (1995) presents. One of these factors seems to be the length of the words, as noted by Zipf (1935) and analyzed by Sigurd et al. (2004).

Zipf (1935) suggests that the length of a word tends to bear an inverse relationship, not necessarily proportionate, to its relative frequency. Sigurd et al. (2004) analyze data from different text genres in English and Swedish and corroborate the hypothesis, showing that longer words tend to be avoided, presumably because they are uneconomic.

Given this evidence, and considering the concern of Twitter users to save space, since the maximum size of each tweet is 140 characters, we investigate whether the length of a hashtag is one of the strictly linguistic factors that influence on their success or failure.

In order to carry out this analysis, we compared the length of the most popular hashtags in each of the bases with the less popular ones. We noticed that the most popular ones are simple, direct and short; on the other hand, among those with little utilization, many are formed by long strings of characters. Table 5 displays preliminary information about the length of hashtags and popularity and shows that hashtags formed by 15 or more characters are not present among the most used tags.

Table 6 lists the average length, in number of characters, of different groups of hashtags, divided according to their positions in the ranking of frequency of each base.

Most common hashtags (number of tweets)	**Most common hashtags with 15 or more characters (number of tweets)**
#michaeljackson (35,861) #michael (27,298) #mj (16,758)	#nothingpersonal (962) #iwillneverforget (912) #thankyoumichael (690)
#swineflu (230,457) #h1n1 (70,693) #swine (12,444)	#swinefluhatesyou (1,056) #crapnamesforpubs (145) #superhappyfunflu (124)
#musicmonday (824,778) #musicmondays (11,770) #music (5,106)	#musicmondayhttp (540) #fatpeoplearesexier (471) #crapurbanlegends (23)

Table 5. Confrontation of most common hashtags and most common 15-character hashtags. In front of each hashtag is given the number of times it was used in tweets of the base.

Topic	**Average length of...**					
	...the *k* most popular hashtags					**...the less popular hashtags**
	***k*=10**	***k*=20**	***k*=30**	***k*=40**	***k*=50**	
MJ	7.1	6.85	7.8	8.02	7.74	10.16
SF	5.3	7.35	7.17	7.2	7.04	10.3
MM	9.5	8.4	7.27	6.4	5.92	11.66

Table 6. Average length of the most and the less popular hashtags. The samples with the less popular hashtags were formed by 50 randomly selected hashtags among those which appeared only in one tweet of each base.

In all of the bases, the average length of the most popular hashtags is considerably lower to the average length of the less popular ones. Figure 4 compares data from Table 6, including information about standard deviation. It is clear that the differences between the lengths of the few most popular tags are not relevant, as the average lengths of the k most popular tags, with k={10,20,30,40,50}, are roughly similar and do not follow a fixed pattern. However, the comparison with 1-tweet hashtags (less popular ones) shows important differences which led us to believe that the length of a hashtag may be an internal factor – or a strictly linguistic factor – that determines the success or the failure of tags on Twitter, even if more accurate study is needed at this point.

This reflects the small number of hashtags composed of complete sentences (such as #mileycometobrazil, #herewegoagain and many others) occupying good positions in the popularity rankings. Their low standard of success can be attributed to some reasons besides their increased length, such as: (1) sentences admit high rate of variation (e.g. #thankyoumichael, #thanksmj, #michaeljacksonthanks), which reduces the frequency of each of the competing forms; (2) sentences are more difficult to memorize, as they may accept different word orders; and (3) in sentences, it seems to be more prone to misspellings (as in #thanktyoumichael), maybe because of the apparent difficulty of reading the terms without the ordinary spaces between them (we believe that it is easier to notice the misspelling in "thankt you michael" than in "thanktyoumichael", though this is an assumption that must be verified through more extensive work in Psycholinguistics and Applied Linguistics).

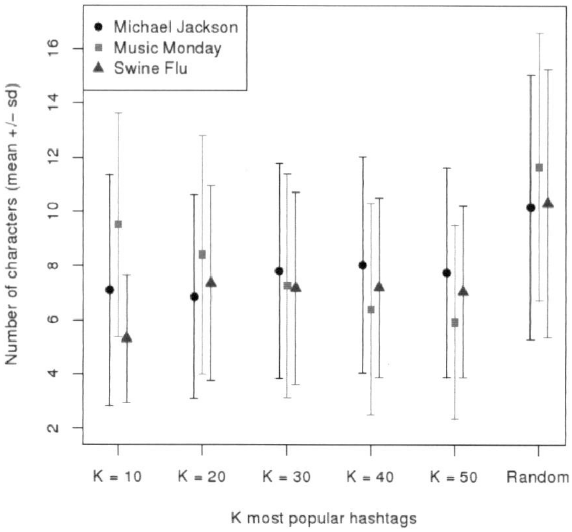

Figure 4. Average number of characters of the most popular hashtags and of a randomly selected sample of 50 less common tags.

7 Underscores in hashtags

We conducted an analysis to check the influence of the only sign allowed in the formation of hashtags besides letters and numbers: the underscore (_). In all the bases, the use of the sign _ led the hashtags to low popularity rankings: #michael_jackson reached position 248 in its base, with only 128 tweets; #swine_flu reached position 67 in its base, with no more than 246 tweets; #music_monday wasn't even used. Table 7 shows the use of sign _ in hashtags. Here, we call a "_-hashtag" any hashtag in which has been used the sign _.

Base	Number of _-hashtags	% of _-hashtags among *i*-tweet hashtags	
		i=2	*i*=10
MJ	251 (1.2%)	89%	97%
SF	155 (0.9%)	87%	97%
MM	143 (0.9%)	89%	98%

Table 7. Distribution of hashtags containing the sign "_".

We can observe that almost all of the _-hashtags have lower positions in the popularity rankings: at least 97% of them are used in 10 or less tweets, which seems to indicate rejection to this sign. Once again, the distributions corresponding to each of the bases are similar, suggesting a uniform behavior across the whole network.

8 Conclusion

This paper examines, through a language-based approach, some issues concerning the formation and the usage of hashtags on Twitter. We proposed that linguistic theory could be used to formulate hypothesis on online systems like Twitter and our analysis showed not only qualitative, but also quantitative similarities between offline and online speech communities.

We revealed interesting aspects about the distribution of hashtags according to their popularity, associating it to the distribution of words in frequency rankings. We also went further on the question suggested by Romero et al. (2011), who proposed to consider what distinguishes a hashtag that spreads widely from one that fails to attract attention: we could find that the tag's length, for example, is one of these factors. This kind of analysis can be a useful tool for tag recommendation systems in different environments, but there are a number of other aspects which can be considered in future work and that can collaborate to the study of human tagging behavior.

References

Breivik, L.E., and Jahr, E.H. (Eds.) 1989. *Language change: Contributions to the study of its causes.* Berlin/New York: Mouton de Gruyter.

Cha, M., Haddadi, H., Benevenuto, F., and Gummadi, K.P. (2010). Measuring user influence in Twitter: The million follower fallacy. *Int'l AAAI Conference on Weblogs and Social Media (ICWSM'10).* Washington DC, USA.

Chew C., and Eysenbach G. 2010. Pandemics in the age of Twitter: Content analysis of tweets during the 2009 H1N1 outbreak. *PLoS ONE 5(11): e14118.* doi: 10.1371/journal.pone.0014118

Easley, D., and Kleinberg, J. 2010. *Networks, crowds, and markets: Reasoning about a highly connected world.* Cambridge: Cambridge University Press.

Kricfalusi, E. 2009. The Twitter hash tag: What is it and how do you use it? Retrieved from http://tinyurl.com/bw85z2

Kwak, H., Lee, C., Park, H., and Moon, S. 2010. What is Twitter, a social network or a news media? *International World Wide Web Conference (WWW 2010).* Raleigh, USA.

Labov, W. 1995. *Principles of linguistic change: Internal factors.* Reprint. Oxford/Cambridge: Blackwell.

Labov, W. 2001. *Principles of linguistic change: Social factors.* Oxford/Cambridge: Blackwell.

Romero, D., Meeder, B., and Kleinberg, J. 2011. Differences in the mechanics of information diffusion across topics: Idioms, political hashtags, and complex contagion on Twitter. *International World Wide Web Conference (WWW 2011).* Hyderabad, India.

Sapir, E. 1921. *Language: An introduction to the study of speech.* New York: Harcourt, Brace and World.

Sigurd, B., Eeg-Olofsson M., and Van de Weijer, J. 2004. World length, sentence length and frequency – Zipf revisited. *Studia Linguistica 58(1),* (pp.37-52). Oxford/Malden: Blackwell.

Silva, L.G. 2006. A dimensão sociolingüística do Atlas Lingüístico do Brasil. *Anais da VIII Semana de Letras da Universidade Federal de Ouro Preto.* Ouro Preto, Brazil: Universidade Federal de Ouro Preto.

Troutman, C., Clark, B., and Goldrick, M. 2008. Social networks and intraspeaker variation during periods of language change. *Proceedings of the 31st Annual Penn Linguistics Colloquium.* (pp.325-338). Philadelphia: University of Pennsylvania.

Twitter, 2010. About Twitter: A few Twitter facts. Retrieved from http://twitter.com/about.

Weinreich, U., Labov, W., and Herzog, M. 1968. Empirical foundations for a theory of language change. In Lehmann W., and Malkiel Y. (Eds.), *Directions for historical linguistics* (pp.97-195). Austin: University of Texas Press.

Zipf, G.K. 1935 (reprinted 1965). *The psycho-biology of language.* Cambridge: MIT Press.

Zipf, G.K. 1949. *Human behavior and the principle of least effort.* Cambridge: Addison-Wesley.

Why is "SXSW" trending? Exploring Multiple Text Sources for Twitter Topic Summarization

Fei Liu[1] **Yang Liu**[1] **Fuliang Weng**[2]
[1]Computer Science Department, The University of Texas at Dallas
[2]Research and Technology Center, Robert Bosch LLC
{feiliu, yangl}@hlt.utdallas.edu[1]
fuliang.weng@us.bosch.com[2]

Abstract

User-contributed content is creating a surge on the Internet. A list of "buzzing topics" can effectively monitor the surge and lead people to their topics of interest. Yet a topic phrase alone, such as "SXSW", can rarely present the information clearly. In this paper, we propose to explore a variety of text sources for summarizing the Twitter topics, including the tweets, normalized tweets via a dedicated tweet normalization system, web contents linked from the tweets, as well as integration of different text sources. We employ the concept-based optimization framework for topic summarization, and conduct both automatic and human evaluation regarding the summary quality. Performance differences are observed for different input sources and types of topics. We also provide a comprehensive analysis regarding the task challenges.

1 Introduction

User contributed content has become a major source of information in the Web 2.0 era. People follow their topics of interest, share their experience or opinions on a variety of interactive platforms, including forums, blogs, microblogs, social networking sites, etc. To keep track of the trends online and suggest topics of interest to the general public, many leading websites provide a "buzzing" service by publishing the current most popular topics on their entrance page and update them regularly, such as the "popular now" column on Bing.com, "trending topics" on Twitter.com, "trending now" on Yahoo.com, Google Trends, and so forth. Often popular topics are in the form of a list of keywords or phrases[1]. Take Twitter.com as an example. Clicking on a trending topic phrase will return a set of relevant Twitter posts (tweets) or web pages. Nonetheless, whether this is a convenient way for users to navigate through the popular topic information is still arguable. For example, when "SXSW" was listed as a trending topic, it seems difficult to understand at the first glance. A condensed topic summary would be extremely helpful for the users before diving into the massive search results to figure out what this topic phrase is about and why it is trending. In this paper, our goal is to generate a short text summary for any given topic phrase. Note that the proposed approach is not limited to trending topics, but can be applied to arbitrary Twitter topics.

There are a lot of differences between tweets and traditional written text that has been widely used for automatic summarization. In Table 1, we show example tweets for the topic "SXSW". The tweets were extracted by searching the Twitter site using the topic phrase as a query. We also provide an excerpt of the linked web content to help understand the topic. The tweets present some unique characteristics:

- All tweets are limited to 140 characters. Some tweets are news headlines from the official media, others are generated by users with various degrees of familiarity with the social media. The resulting tweets can be very different regarding the text quality and word usage.

[1]They are referred to as topic phrases hereafter, with no distinction between keywords and key phrases.

Twitter Topic: "SXSW"	
Twts	I wish I could go to SXSW... I will, one day! *http://sxsw.com/*
	RT @user123: SXSW Film Round-Up: Documentaries *http://bit.ly/fg033b*
	@user456 yo.whats good,i met u at sxsw, talkin bout that feature.I was gonna see about sending u a few beats.u lookin for only original?
Web Cont	The South by Southwest (SXSW) Conferences & Festivals offer the unique convergence of original music, independent films, and emerging technologies...*(http://sxsw.com/)*

Table 1: Example tweets and an excerpt of the linked web content for Twitter topic "SXSW".

- Tweets lack structure information, contain various ill-formed sentences and grammatical errors. There are lots of noisy nonstandard tokens, such as abbreviations ("feelin" for "feeling"), substitutions ("Pr1mr0se" for "Primrose"), emoticons, etc.
- Twitter invented its own markup language. "@user" is used to reply to a specific user or call for attentions. The hashtag "#topic" aims to assign a topic label to the tweet, and is frequently employed by the twitter users.
- Tweets frequently contain embedded URLs that direct users to other online content, such as news web pages, blogs, organization homepages (Wu et al., 2011). According to Twitter's news release in September 2010 (Rao, 2010), 25% of tweets contain an URL. These linked web pages provide a much richer source of information than is possible in the 140-character tweet.

These Twitter-specific characteristics may pose challenges to the automatic summarization systems for identifying the essential information. In this paper, we focus on two such characteristics that are not studied in previous literature, the web content link and the non-standard tokens in tweets. Specifically, we ask two questions: (1) Is the web content linked from the tweets useful for summarization? Can we integrate different text sources, including the tweets and linked web pages, to generate more informative Twitter topic summaries? (2) what is the effect of nonstandard tokens on summarization performance? Will the summaries be improved if the noisy tweets were pre-normalized into standard English sentences? We investigate these two questions under a concept-based summarization framework using integer linear programming (ILP). We utilize text input that has various quality and is originated from multiple sources, and thoroughly analyze the resulting summaries using both automatic and human evaluation metrics.

2 Related Work

There is not much previous work on summarizing the Twitter topics. Most previous summarization literature focused on the written text domain, as driven by the annual evaluation tracks of the DUC (Document Understanding Conference) and TAC (Text Analysis Conference). To some extent, Twitter topic summarization is related to spoken document summarization, since both tasks deal with the conversational text that is contributed by multiple participants and contains lots of ill-formed sentences, colloquial expressions, nonstandard word tokens or high word error rate, etc. To summarize the spoken text, (Zechner, 2002) aimed to address problems related to disfluencies, extraction units, cross-speaker coherence, etc. (Maskey and Hirschberg, 2005; Murray et al., 2006; Galley, 2006; Xie et al., 2008; Liu and Liu, 2010a) incorporated lexical, structural, speaker, and discourse cues to generate textual summaries for broadcast news and meeting conversations.

For microblog summarization, (Sharifi et al., 2010a) proposed a phrase reinforcement (PR) algorithm to summarize the Twitter topic in one sentence. The algorithm builds a word graph using the topic phrase as the root node; each word node is weighted in proportion to its distance to the root and the corresponding phrase frequency. The summary sentence is selected as one of the highest weighted paths in the graph. (Sharifi et al., 2010b; Inouye, 2010) introduced a hybrid TF-IDF approach to extract one- or multiple-sentence summary for each topic. Sentences were ranked according to the average TF-IDF score of the consisting words; top weighted sentences were iteratively extracted, but excluding those that have high cosine similarity with the existing summary sentences. They showed the Hybrid TF-IDF approach performs constantly better than the PR algorithm and other traditional summarization systems. Our approach of summarizing the Twitter topics is different from the above studies in that, we focus on exploring richer information sources (such as the online web content) and investigating effect of non-standard tokens. There are also studies working on visualizing Twitter topics by identifying a set of topic phrases and presenting the related tweets to users (O'Connor et al., 2010; Marcus et al., 2011). Our proposed approach can be beneficial to these systems by providing informative topic summaries generated from rich text sources.

3 Data Collection

We collected 5,537 topic phrases and the reference topic descriptions by crawling the Twitter.com and WhatTheTrend.com simultaneously during the period of Aug 22th, 2010 to Oct 30th, 2010 (about 70 days). The Twitter API was queried every 5 minutes for the current top ten trending topics. For each of these topics, a search query was submitted to the Twitter Search API to retrieve only English tweets related to this topic. If any tweet contains embedded URLs linked to the other web pages, the contents of these web pages were retrieved. For each topic, we limit the maximum number of retrieved tweets to 5,000 and webpages to 100. An example is shown in Table 1 for a topic phrase, some related tweets, and an excerpt of the linked webpage. WhatTheTrend API provides short topic descriptions contributed and constantly updated by the Twitter users. There is also a manually assigned category tag for each topic phrase. We found the top categories among the collected topics are "Entertainment (29.26%)", "Sports (25.58%)", and "Meme (15.69%, pointless babble)". We divided the collected topics into two groups: the general topics (e.g., "Chilean miners", "MTV VMA") and the hashtag topics that start with the "#" (e.g., "#top10rappers", "#octoberwish").

To generate reference summaries for the Twitter topics, two human annotators were asked to pick the topic descriptions/sentences (collected from WhatTheTrend.com) that are appropriate and valuable to be included in the summary. This is performed on a selected set of 1,511 topics with both trending duration and number of tweets greater than our predefined thresholds. For each of the topic sentences, we ask the annotators to label its category: (1) the sentence is a general description of the topic; (2) the sentence is trying to explain why the topic is trending; (3) it is hard to tell the difference. Overall, the two annotators have good agreement (Kappa = 0.67) regarding whether or not to include a sentence in the summary. Among the selected summary sentences, 22.58% of them were assigned with conflicting purpose tags such as (1) or (2). To form a reference summary, we concatenate all the topic sentences selected by both annotators. Since some reference descriptions are simply repetition of others with very minor changes, we reduce the duplicates by iteratively removing the oldest sentences if all the consisting words are covered by the remaining sentence collection, until no sentence can be removed. On average, the reference summary for general and hashtag topics contains 44 and 40 words respectively.

4 Summarization System

For each of the topic phrases, our goal is to generate a short textual summary that can best convey the main ideas of the topic contents. We explore and compare multiple text sources as summarization input, including the user-contributed tweets, web contents linked from the tweets, as well as combination of the two sources. The concept-based optimization approach (Gillick et al., 2009; Xie et al., 2009; Murray et al., 2010) was employed for selecting informative summary sentences and minimizing the redundancy. Note that our focus of this paper is not developing new summarization systems, but rather utilizing and integrating different text sources for generating more informative Twitter topic summaries.

4.1 Concept-based Optimization Framework

Concept-based summarization approach first extracts a set of important concepts for each topic, then selects a collection of sentences that can cover as many important concepts as possible, while within the specified length limit. This idea is realized using the integer linear programming-based (ILP) optimization framework, with objective function set to maximize the sum of the weighted concepts:

$$\max \quad \sum_i w_i c_i$$

where c_i is a binary variable indicating whether the concept i is covered by the summary; w_i is the weight assigned to c_i.

We enforce two sets of length constraints to the summary: sentence- or word-based. Sentence constraint requires the total number of selected summary sentences to not to exceed a length limit L_1; while word constraint requires the total words of selected sentences not to exceed length limit L_2. These two constraints are:

$$\sum_j s_j < L_1 \quad or \quad \sum_j l_j s_j < L_2$$

where s_j is a binary variable indicating whether sentence j was selected in the summary; l_j represents the number of words in s_j.

Further, we connect concept i with sentence j using two sets of constraints. For all the sentences that contain concept i, if any sentence was selected in the summary, the concept i should be covered by the summary; reversely, if concept i was covered by the summary, at least one of the sentences containing concept i should be selected.

$$\forall i \quad c_i \leq \sum_j o_{ij} s_j$$

$$\forall i, j \quad c_i \geq o_{ij} s_j$$

where the binary variable o_{ij} is used to indicate whether concept i exists in sentence j.

The concepts are selected by extracting n-grams (n=1, 2, 3) from the input documents corresponding to each topic. Similar to (Xie et al., 2009), we remove (1) n-grams that appear only once in the documents; (2) n-grams that have a consisting word with inverse document frequency (IDF) value lower than a threshold; (3) n-grams that are enclosed by higher order n-grams with the same frequency. These filters are designed to exclude insignificant n-grams from the concept set. The IDF scores were calculated from a large background corpus corresponding to the input text source, using individual sentences or tweets as pseudo-documents; words with low IDF scores (such as stopwords) tend to appear in many sentences and therefore should be removed from the concept set. We assign a weight w_i to an n-gram concept as follows:

$$w_i = tf(ngram_i) \times n \times \max_j \; idf(w_{ij})$$

where $tf(ngram_i)$ is the term frequency of $ngram_i$ in the input document of the topic; n denotes the order of $ngram_i$; w_{ij} are the consisting words of $ngram_i$; $idf(w_{ij})$ represents IDF value of word w_{ij}. This approach aims to extract n-grams that appear frequently in each topic, but do not appear frequently in a large background corpus. The weights are also biased towards longer n-grams since they carry more information.

4.2 Summarization Input

In this section, we explore different text sources as input to the summarization system. Different from previous studies that take input from a single text source, we propose to utilize both the user-contributed tweets and the linked web contents for Twitter topic summarization, since these two sources provide very different text quality and may contain complementary information regarding the topic. These text sources also pose great challenges to the summarization system: the tweets are short and extremely noisy; while the online contents linked from the tweets may have vastly different layouts and contain a variety of information.

4.2.1 Original Tweets

As shown in Table 1, the initially collected tweets are very noisy. They are passed through a set of preprocessors to remove non-ascii characters, HTML special characters, URLs, emoticons, punctuation marks, retweet tags (RT @user), etc. We also remove the reply (@) and hashtag (#) tokens that do not carry important syntactic roles (such as in the subject or object position) by using a set of regular expressions. These preprocessed tweets are sorted by date and taken as the first input source to the summarization system (denoted by "OrigTweets").

4.2.2 Normalized Tweets

The original tweets contain various nonstandard word tokens. In Table 2, we list the possible token categories and corresponding examples. We hypothesize that normalizing these nonstandard tokens into standard English words and using the normalized tweets as input can help boost the summarization performance.

We developed a twitter message normalization system based on the noisy-channel framework and a proposed letter transformation model (Liu et al.,

Category	Example
(1) abbreviation	tgthr, weeknd, shudnt
(2) phonetic sub w/- or w/o digit	4got, sumbody, kulture
(3) graphemic sub w/- or w/o digit	t0gether, h3r3, 5top, doinq
(4) typographic error	thimg, macam
(5) stylistic variation	betta, hubbie, cutie
(6) letter repetition	pleeeaas, togtherrr
(7) any combination of (1) to (6)	luvvvin, 2moro, m0rnin

Table 2: Nonstandard token categories and examples.

2011). Given a noisy tweet T, our goal is to normalize it into a standard English word sequence S. Under the noisy channel model, this is equivalent to finding the sequence $\hat{S}$ that maximizes $p(S|T)$:

$$\hat{S} = \arg\max_S p(S|T) = \arg\max_S (\prod_i p(T_i|S_i))p(S)$$

where we assume that each non-standard token T_i is dependent on only one English word S_i, that is, we are not considering acronyms (e.g., "bbl" for "be back later") in this study. $p(S)$ can be calculated using a language model (LM). We formulate the process of generating a nonstandard token T_i from dictionary word S_i using a letter transformation model, and use the model confidence as the probability $p(T_i|S_i)$. This transformation process will be learned automatically through a sequence labeling framework. To form a nonstandard token, each letter in the dictionary word can be labeled with: (a) one of the 0-9 digits; (b) one of the 26 characters including itself; (c) the null character "-"; (d) a letter combination. We integrate character-, phonetic-, and syllable-level features in the model that can effectively characterize the formation process of nonstandard tokens. In general, the letter transformation approach will handle the nonstandard tokens listed in Table 2 yet without explicitly categorizing them. The proposed system also achieved robust performance using the automatically collected training word pairs. On a test set of 3,802 distinct nonstandard tokens collected from Twitter, our system achieved 68.88% 1-best normalization word accuracy and 78.27% 3-best accuracy.

We identify the nonstandard tokens that need to be normalized using the following criteria: (1) it is not in the CMU dictionary[2]; (2) it does not contain capitalized letter; (3) it appears infrequently in the topic (less than a threshold); (4) it is not a popular chat acronyms (such as "lol", "omg"); (5) it contains letters/digits/apostrophe, but should not be numbers only. These criteria are designed to avoid normalizing the named entities, frequently appearing out-of-vocabulary terms (such as "itunes"), chat acronyms, usernames, and hashtags. The selected nonstandard tokens in the original tweets will be replaced by the system generated 1-best candidate word. Note that we do not discriminate the context when replacing each nonstandard token. This will be addressed in the future work. We use these normalized tweets as a second source of summarization input and name them "NormTweets".

4.2.3 Linked Web Contents

For each Twitter topic, we collect a set of web pages linked by the topic tweets and use them as another source of summarization input. For each topic, we select up to n (n = 10) URLs that appear most frequently in the topic tweets and infrequently across different Twitter topics. This scheme is similar to the TF-IDF measure. This way we can select the salient URLs for each topic while avoiding the spam URLs. The contents of these URLs were collected and only distinct web pages were retained. We use an HTML parser[3] to extract the textual contents, and perform sentence segmentation (Reynar and Ratnaparkhi, 1997) on the parsed web pages. All the pages corresponding to the same topic were sorted by the date they were first cited in the tweets. These web pages were taken as another input text source for the summarization system, denoted as "Web".

4.2.4 Combining Tweets and Web Contents

We expect that taking advantage of both tweets and linked web contents would benefit the topic summarization system. Consolidating the distinct text sources may help boost the weight of key concepts and eliminate the spam information. As a preliminary study, we investigate concatenating either the original tweets or the normalized tweets with the linked web pages as input to the concept-based summarization system. This results in two inputs "Web + OrigTweets" and "Web + NormTweets". We will explore other ways of combining the two text

[2]http://www.speech.cs.cmu.edu/cgi-bin/cmudict

[3]http://jericho.htmlparser.net/docs/index.html

sources in future work.

5 Experiments

5.1 Experimental Setup

Among the collected topics, we select 500 general topics (such as "Chilean miners") and 50 hashtag topics (such as "#octoberwish", "#wheniwasakid") for experimentation. On average, a general topic contains 1673 tweets and 3.43 extracted linked web pages; while a hashtag topic contains 3316 tweets but does not have meaningful linked web pages.

The concept-based optimization system was configured to extract a collection of sentences/tweets for each topic, using either the sentence- or word-constraint (denoted as "#Sent" and "#Word"). We opt to set individual length constraint for each topic rather than using a uniform length limit for all the topics, since the topics can be very different in length and duration. We use the number of sentences/words in the reference summary as the sentence/word constraint for each topic. Note that in practice this reference summary length information may not be available. We use the length constraints obtained from the reference summary in this exploratory study, since our focus is to first evaluate if twitter trending summarization is feasible, and what are the effects of different information sources and non-standard tokens. For a comparison to our approach, we implement the Hybrid TF-IDF approach in (Sharifi et al., 2010b; Inouye, 2010) as a baseline using "OrigTweets" as input. For the baseline, the summary length is altered according to the sentence- or word-constraint. The last summary tweet is cut in the middle if it exceeds the word limit.

The ROUGE-1 F-scores (Lin, 2004) are used to measure the n-gram (n=1) overlap between the system summaries and reference summaries. Since the ROUGE scores may not correlate well with the human judgments (Liu and Liu, 2010b), we also performed human evaluation by asking annotators to score both the system and reference summaries regarding the linguistic quality and content responsiveness, in the hope this will benefit future research in this direction.

5.2 Automatic Evaluation

We present the results (ROUGE-1 F-measure) for the general topics in Table 3. ROUGE-2 and ROUGE-4 scores show similar trends and thus are not presented. Five different text sources were exploited as the system inputs, as described in Section 4.2. To measure the quality of the input for summarization, we also include reference summary coverage score in the table, defined as the percentage of words in the reference summary that are covered by the input text source. When using tweets as input, we also investigate whether we should apply tweet normalization before or after the summarization process, that is "pre-normalization" (using "NormTweets" as input), or "post-normalization" (using "OrigTweets" as input, and rendering the normalized summary tweets).

General Topics		R-1 F(%)		RefSum
Input Source	Render	#Sent	#Word	Cov(%)
OrigTweets	Orig	29.53	30.21	94.81
	Norm	29.41	30.21	94.81
NormTweets	Norm	29.69	30.35	94.60
Web		24.32	25.07	63.74
Web + OrigTweets		29.58	30.44	95.37
Web + NormTweets		29.66	**30.54**	95.16
OrigTweets (Sharifi et al., 2010b)		24.37	25.68	94.81

Table 3: ROUGE-1 F-measure and reference summary coverage scores for general topics.

Compared to the Hybrid TF-IDF approach (Sharifi et al., 2010b; Inouye, 2010), our system performs significantly better ($p < 0.05$) according to the paired t-test; however, we also notice the ROUGE scores are lower compared to summarization in other text domains. This indicates that Twitter topic summarization is very challenging. Comparing the two constraints used in the concept-based optimization framework, we found that the word constraint performs constantly better for the general topics. This is natural since the word constraint tightly bounds the length of the system output, while the sentence constraint is relatively loose. For the different sources, we notice using linked web pages alone yields worse summarization performance, as well as lower reference summary coverage; however, when combined with the tweets, there is a slight increase in the coverage scores, and sometimes improved summarization results. This suggests that the linked web pages can contain extra useful information for generating summaries. Regarding normalization, results show that the "pre-normalization" (using normalized tweets as input) can generally improve the summary tweet selection. For general topics, the best performance was achieved by combining the normalized tweets and linked web pages as input source and using the word-level constraint.

Hashtag Topics		R-1 F(%)		RefSum
Input Source	Render	#Sent	#Word	Cov(%)
OrigTweets	Orig	9.08	7.19	93.93
	Norm	9.09	7.16	93.93
NormTweets	Norm	**9.35**	7.14	93.71
OrigTweets (Sharifi et al., 2010b)		7.03	7.72	93.93

Table 4: ROUGE-1 F-measure and reference summary coverage scores for hashtag topics.

Results for hashtag topics were shown in Table 4 using tweets as input (there are no linked webpages for these topics). We notice the reference coverage scores are satisfying, yet the system output barely matches the reference summaries (very low ROUGE-1 scores). Looking at the reference and system generated summaries for the hashtag topics, we found the system output is more specific (e.g., "#octoberwish everything goes well."), while the reference summaries are often very general (e.g., "people tweeting about their wishes for October."). The human annotators also noted that most hashtag topics (such as "#octoberwish", "#wheniwasakid") are self-explainable and may require special attention to redefine an appropriate summary. Using sentence constraints yields better performance than word-based one, with larger performance difference than that for the general topics. We found the word-constraint summaries tend to include tweets that are very short and noisy. Our system with sentence-based length constraint also significantly outperforms the Hybrid TF-IDF approach (Sharifi et al., 2010b; Inouye, 2010). For hashtag topics, the best performance was achieved using the "pre-normalization" with sentence constraint.

For an analysis, we generate oracle system performance by using the reference summaries to extract a set of unweighted concepts to use in the ILP optimization framework for sentences/tweets selection. This results in 61.76% ROUGE-1 F-score for the general topics and 40.34% for the hashtag topics, indicating abundant space for future improvement. We also notice that though there is some performance gain using normalized tweets and linked web contents, the improvement is not statistically significant as compared to using the original tweets. Upon closer examination, we found the normalization system replaced 1.08% and 1.8% of the total word tokens for the general and hashtag topics respectively; these tokens spread in 13.12% and 16.85% of the total tweets. The relatively small percentage of the normalized tokens partly explains the marginal performance gain when using the normalized tweets as input. Similarly for linked web content, though it contains some sentences that can provide more details of the topic, but they can also take more space in the summary as compared to the short and condensed tweets. Therefore using the combined tweets and linked webpages does not significantly outperform using just the tweets.

5.3 Human Evaluation

	General			Hashtag	
	Tweet	Web	Ref	Tweet	Ref
Gram.	3.13	**3.42**	4.52	3.04	4.24
NRedun.	3.93	**4.64**	4.30	4.82	3.62
Clarity	**4.07**	3.91	4.77	4.06	4.60
Focus	**3.64**	3.03	4.75	3.22	4.72
Content	2.82	2.55	n/a	2.60	n/a
ExtraInfo	n/a	2.63	n/a	n/a	n/a

Table 5: Linguistic quality, content coverage, and usefulness scores judged by human assessors.

We ask two human annotators to manually evaluate the system and reference summaries regarding the readability and content coverage. Readability includes grammaticality, non-redundancy, referential clarity, and focus; content coverage was evaluated for system summaries against the reference summary. The annotators were also asked to rate the "Web" summaries regarding whether they provided extra useful topic information on top of the "Tweet" summary. 50 general topics and 25 hashtag topics were randomly selected for assessment. The "Tweet" and "Web" summaries were generated using the original tweets and linked web pages with word constraint for general topics, and sentence constraint for hashtag topics. Each of the assessors was

General Topic: "3PAR"	
RefSum	Dell Inc. and Hewlett-Packard Co. are both bidding for storage device maker 3Par Inc. 3Par jumped 21 percent after Hewlett- Packard Co. offered $30 a share for the company.
TweetSum	Dell ups 3Par offer yet again, to $27 per share Dell Raises 3par Offer to Match HP Bid Dell Matches HP's Offer for 3Par, Boosting Bid to $1.8 Billion
WebSum	Dell Matches HP's $27 Offer, Is Accepted by 3PAR. 3PAR has accepted an increased acquisition offer from Dell of US$27 per share, matching Hewlett-Packard's earlier raised bid.

Hashtag Topic: "#wheniwasakid"	
RefSum	when i was a kid.... people are sharing there best (good or bad) memories from childhood. People reminise the wonderful times about being a kid.
TweetSum	#whenIwasakid getting wasted meant eating all the ice cream and candy you could until you puked! #whenIWasAKid Apple & Blackberry were fruits not phones.

Table 6: Example system and reference summaries for both general and hashtag topics.

asked to judge all the summaries and assign a score for each criterion on a 1 to 5 Likert scale (5 being the best quality). The average scores of the two assessors were presented in Table 5.

For general topics, the "Web" summaries outperform the "Tweet" summaries on both grammaticality and non-redundancy, confirming the advantage of using the high-quality linked web pages. The referential clarity and focus scores of the "Web" summaries are not very high, since the summary sentences were extracted simultaneously from several web pages, and the system subjects to similar challenges as in multi-document summarization. The content coverage scores of both system summaries seem to correlate well with the ROUGE-1 F-measure, with a higher score for "Tweet" summaries. The assessors also rated that 48% of the "Web" summaries contain "Somewhat Useful" extra topic information, and 21% are "Very Useful". Note that this could be just because of the inherent difference of the two summaries, regardless of the input source, but in general we believe the linked web pages (such as the news documents) can provide more detailed and coherent stories as compared to the 140-character tweets. For hashtag topics, the "Tweet" summaries yield worse grammaticality and focus scores, but have very high non-redundancy score. On the contrary, the reference summaries often contain redundant information. The content match score between the system and reference summaries (2.6) does not seem to reflect the ROUGE scores. We hypothesize that even though the specificity of the two summaries is different, the assessors may still think the system summaries match the reference ones to some extent. A larger scale human evaluation is needed to study the correlation between human and automatic evaluation.

5.4 Discussions

We show an example of reference and system generated summaries for a general and a hashtag topic in Table 6, and summarize some challenges for this summarization task below:

- **Gold standard summaries are difficult and time-consuming to obtain.** The reference descriptions from WhatTheTrend.com were created by Twitter users, which vary a lot in word usage and would be unavoidably biased to the information available in Twitter. The user-contributed descriptions may also contain spam descriptions, repetitions, nonstandard tokens, etc. It would be better to have a concise non-redundant sentence collection for developing future summarization systems. In particular, hashtag topics need special attention. They account for 40% of the total trending topics in 2010 according to the statistics in WhatTheTrend.com[4]. Yet there still lacks standard definition regarding a good hashtag summary. From the example topic "#wheniwasakid" in Table 6, we can see they are very different in nature from general topics, thus future efforts are needed to define an appropriate summary.

[4]http://yearinreview.whatthetrend.com/

- **Evaluation issues.** Word based evaluation measures will rarely consider semantic relatedness between concepts, or name entity variations, such as "Hewlett-Packard" vs. "HP", "Dell ups 3Par offer" vs. "Dell Raises 3par Offer", etc. When comparing the system summaries with short human-written reference summaries, the word overlap varies a lot for different human summarizers.

- **Dynamically changing topics/events.** Some general topics are related to events that are constantly changing. Take the "3PAR" topic in Table 6 as an example, where two companies take turns to raise the bid for 3Par Inc. A good topic summary should be able to develop a series of sub-events and show the topic evolving process.

6 Conclusion

In this paper, we proposed to explore a variety of text sources for summarizing the Twitter topics. We employed the concept-based optimization framework with multiple input text sources to generate the summaries. We conducted both automatic and human evaluation regarding the summary quality. Better performance is observed when using the normalized tweets as input, indicating special treatment should be performed before feeding the noisy tweets to the summarization system. We also found the linked web contents can provide extra useful topic information. In future work, we will compare our system with other dedicated microblog summarization systems, as well as address some of the challenges identified in this study.

Acknowledgments

This work is partly supported by NSF award IIS-0845484. Any opinions expressed in this work are those of the authors and do not necessarily reflect the views of NSF.

References

Michel Galley. 2006. A skip-chain conditional random field for ranking meeting utterances by importance. In *Proc. of EMNLP*.

Dan Gillick, Korbinian Riedhammer, Benoit Favre, and Dilek Hakkani-Tür. 2009. A global optimization framework for meeting summarization. In *Proc. of ICASSP*.

David Inouye. 2010. Multiple post microblog summarization. *REU Research Final Report*.

Chin-Yew Lin. 2004. ROUGE: A package for automatic evaluation of summaries. In *Workshop on Text Summarization Branches Out*.

Fei Liu and Yang Liu. 2010a. Exploring speaker characteristics for meeting summarization. In *Proc. of INTERSPEECH*.

Feifan Liu and Yang Liu. 2010b. Exploring correlation between ROUGE and human evaluation on meeting summaries. *IEEE Transactions on Audio, Speech, and Language Processing*, 18(1):187–196.

Fei Liu, Fuliang Weng, Bingqing Wang, and Yang Liu. 2011. Insertion, deletion, or substitution? Normalizing text messages without pre-categorization nor supervision. In *Proc. of ACL-HLT*.

Adam Marcus, Michael S. Bernstein, Osama Badar, David R. Karger, Samuel Madden, and Robert C. Miller. 2011. TwitInfo: Aggregating and visualizing microblogs for event exploration. In *Proc. of CHI*.

Sameer Maskey and Julia Hirschberg. 2005. Comparing lexical, acoustic/prosodic, structural and discourse features for speech summarization. In *Proc. of Eurospeech*.

Gabriel Murray, Steve Renals, Jean Carletta, and Johanna Moore. 2006. Incorporating speaker and discourse features into speech summarization. In *Proc. of HLT-NAACL*.

Gabriel Murray, Giuseppe Carenini, and Raymond Ng. 2010. Interpretation and transformation for abstracting conversations. In *Proc. of NAACL*.

Brendan O'Connor, Michel Krieger, and David Ahn. 2010. Tweetmotif: Exploratory search and topic summarization for twitter. In *Proc. of the International AAAI Conference on Weblogs and Social Media*.

Leena Rao. 2010. Twitter seeing 90 million tweets per day, 25 percent contain links. *http://techcrunch.com/2010/09/14/twitter-seeing-90-million-tweets-per-day/*.

Jeffrey C. Reynar and Adwait Ratnaparkhi. 1997. A maximum entropy approach to identifying sentence boundaries. In *Proc. of the Fifth Conference on Applied Natural Language Processing*.

Beaux Sharifi, Mark-Anthony Hutton, and Jugal Kalita. 2010a. Summarizing microblogs automatically. In *Proc. of HLT/NAACL*.

Beaux Sharifi, Mark-Anthony Hutton, and Jugal K. Kalita. 2010b. Experiments in microblog summarization. In *Proc. of IEEE Second International Conference on Social Computing*.

Shaomei Wu, Jake M. Hofman, Winter A. Mason, and Duncan J. Watts. 2011. Who says what to whom on twitter. In *Proc. of WWW*.

Shasha Xie, Yang Liu, and Hui Lin. 2008. Evaluating the effectiveness of features and sampling in extractive meeting summarization. In *Proc. of IEEE Workshop on Spoken Language Technology*.

Shasha Xie, Benoit Favre, Dilek Hakkani-Tür, and Yang Liu. 2009. Leveraging sentence weights in a concept-based optimization framework for extractive meeting summarization. In *Proc. of INTERSPEECH*.

Klaus Zechner. 2002. Automatic summarization of open-domain multiparty dialogues in diverse genres. *Computational Linguistics*, 28(4):447–485.

Language use as a reflection of socialization in online communities

Dong Nguyen
Carnegie Mellon University
Language Technologies Institute
Pittsburgh, PA 15213
dongn@cs.cmu.edu

Carolyn P. Rosé
Carnegie Mellon University
Language Technologies Institute
Pittsburgh, PA 15213
cprose@cs.cmu.edu

Abstract

In this paper we investigate the connection between language and community membership of long time community participants through computational modeling techniques. We report on findings from an analysis of language usage within a popular online discussion forum with participation of thousands of users spanning multiple years. We find community norms of long time participants that are characterized by forum specific jargon and a style that is highly informal and shows familiarity with specific other participants and high emotional involvement in the discussion. We also find quantitative evidence of persistent shifts in language usage towards these norms across users over the course of the first year of community participation. Our observed patterns suggests language stabilization after 8 or 9 months of participation.

1 Introduction

In this paper we use text mining and machine learning methodologies as lenses through which to understand the connection between language use and community membership in online communities. Specifically we examine an online medical support community called breastcancer.org. We present analyses of data from an active online community with the goal of uncovering the connection between language and online community membership. In particular, we will look at language changes that occur over time as people continue to participate in an online community. Consistent with the Communities of Practice theory of participation within a community (Lave and Wenger, 1991), we find increasing conformity to community norms within the first year of participation that then stabilizes as participants continue their involvement in the community.

Within the Communities of Practice view, socialization into a community begins with peripheral participation, during which individuals have the opportunity to observe community norms. Lave and Wenger's theory has been applied to both online and face-to-face communities. In an online community, observing community norms begins with lurking and reading messages before an initial post. This is termed legitimate peripheral participation, and it is during this stage that potential new members observe community norms in action. With an initial post, a user embarks upon the path of centripetal participation, as they are taking steps towards core participation.

Becoming a core member of a community means adopting community norms. Persistent language changes occur as an accumulation of local accommodation effects (Labov, 2010a; Labov, 2010b). The extent of the adoption reflects the commitment to community membership. Thus, as an individual progressively moves from the periphery of a community towards the core, their behavior will progressively grow towards conformity with these norms, although total conformity very rarely occurs. The quantitative analysis we present in the form of a regression model is consistent with this theoretical perspective and allows us to see what centripetal participation and core participation look like within the breastcancer.org community. We are able to test the robustness of these observations by using the extent of conformity to community norms as a predictor of how long a member has been actively participating in an online community. We will present results from this predictive analysis as part of the quantitative evidence we provide in support of this model of community participation.

Patterns of local accommodation and of long time language change within communities have been extensively studied in the field of variationist sociolinguistics. However, with respect to online communities in particular, recent research has looked at accommodation (Danescu-Niculescu-Mizil et al., 2011; Nguyen et al., 2010) and some shorter term language changes (i.e., over a period of a few months). However, longitudinal analyses of language change spanning long time periods (i.e., more than a few months) in online communities as we present in this paper have been largely absent from the literature. Typically, long term language change in sociolinguistics requires reconstructing the past from the present using age grading techniques, since a comprehensive historical record is typically absent (Labov, 2010a; Labov, 2010b). Online communities present a unique opportunity to study long term language change from a much more comprehensive historical record of a community's development.

In the remainder of the paper, we first review prior work on computational models of accommodation and language change. We then present a qualitative view of communication within the breastcancer.org community. We then present two quantitative analyses, one that explores language change in the aggregate, and another that tests the robustness of findings from the first analysis with a regression model that allows us to predict how long a member has been active within the community. We conclude with discussion and future work.

2 Related work

For decades, research under the heading of Social Accommodation Theory (Giles et al., 1973) has attempted to layer a social interpretation on patterns of linguistic variation. This extensive line of research has provided ample quantitative evidence that people adjust their language within interactions, sometimes to build solidarity or liking, and other times to differentiate themselves from others (Eckert and Rickford, 2001).

In this line of work, people have often looked at accommodation in small discussion groups and dyadic conversation pairs. For example, Gonzales et al. (2010) analyzed style matching in small group discussions, and used it to predict cohesiveness and task performance in the groups. Scissors et al. (2009) analyzed conversational pairs playing a social dilemma game and interacting through an instant messenger. They found that certain patterns of high linguistic similarity characterize high trusting pairs. Niederhoffer and Pennebaker (2002) found linguistic style matching both at the conversation level and locally at a turn-by-turn level in dyadic conversations. Paolillo (2001) looked at the connection between linguistic variation and strong and weak ties in an Internet Relay Chat channel. Nguyen et al. (2010) found accommodation effects in an online political forum that contains discussions between people with different political viewpoints. Recently, Danescu-Niculescu-Mizil et al. (2011) showed that accommodation was also present in Twitter conversations.

Lam (2008) gives an overview of work on language socialization in online communities. We know that persistent language changes over long time periods are the accumulated result of local accommodations that occur within short-term contexts for social reasons (Labov, 2010a; Labov, 2010b). However, the process through which individuals adopt the language practices of online communities has been barely explored so far. One example of investigation within this scope is the work of Postmes et al. (2000), in which we find analysis of the formation of group norms in a computer-mediated communication setting. Specifically, they found that small groups were formed during the process and communication norms including language usage patterns were present within those groups. Over time, conformity to these norms increased. Similarly, Cassell and Tversky (2005) looked at evolution of language patterns in an online community. In this work, the participants were students from around the world participating in the Junior Summit forum '98. Cassell and Tversky found that participants converged on style, topics, goals and strategies. Analyses were computed using word frequencies of common classes (such as self references) and

Table 1: Statistics dataset.

Posts	1,562,590
Threads	68,226
Users (at least one post)	31,307
Time-span	Oct 2002 - Jan 2011

manual coding. Huffaker et al. (2006) examined a subset of the same data. When comparing consecutive weeks over a 6 week time period, they found that the language diverged. They hypothesized that this was caused by external events leading to the introduction of new words.

Our research differs from the research by Cassell and Tversky (2005), Huffaker et al. (2006) and Postmes et al. (2000) in several respects. For example, in all of this work, participants joined the community simultaneously at the inception of the community. In contrast, our community of inquiry has evolved over time, with members joining intermittently throughout the history of the community. Additionally, our analysis spans much more time, specifically 2 years of data rather than 3 or 4 months. Thus, this research addresses a different question from the way community norms are first established at the inception of a community. In contrast, what we investigate is how new users are socialized into an existing community in which norms have already been established prior to their arrival.

We are not the first researchers to study our community of inquiry (Jha and Elhadad, 2010). However, prior work on data from this forum was focused on predicting the cancer stage of a patient rather than issues related to language change that we investigate.

3 Data description

We analyze one of the largest breast cancer forums on the web (http://community.breastcancer.org/). All posts and user profiles of the forum were crawled in January 2011.

The forum serves as a platform for many different kinds of interactions, and serving the needs of a variety of types of users. For example, a large proportion of users only join to ask some medical questions, and therefore do not stay active long. In fact, we find that a lot of users (12,349) only post in the first week after their registration. The distribution of number of weeks between a user's last post and registration date follows a power law. However, besides these short-term users, we also find a large number of users who appear to be looking for more social involvement and continue to participate for years, even after their disease is in remission.

This distinction in types of users is reflected in the forum structure. The forum is well organized, containing over 60 subforums targeting different topics. Besides specific subforums targeting medical topics (such as '*Stage I and II Breast Cancer*' and '*Radiation Therapy - Before, During and After*'), there are subforums for certain population groups (such as '*Canadian Breast Cancer Survivors*' and '*Singles with breast cancer*'), for social purposes (such as '*Growing our Friendships After Treatment*', '*Get Togethers*', and '*CyberSisters Photo Album*') and non cancer related purposes (such as '*Humor and Games*'). In many of the subforums there are specific threads that foster the formation of small sub communities, for example threads for people who started chemotherapy in a certain month.

In the data we find community norms of long time participants that are characterized by forum specific jargon and a style that is highly informal and shows familiarity with specific other participants and high emotional involvement in the discussion. We infer that the forum specific jargon is distinct from what we would find in those users outside of it, in that that there are places in the forum explaining commonly used abbreviations to new users. We also observe posts within threads where users ask about certain abbreviations used in previous posts. Some of these abbreviations are cancer related and also used in places other than the forum, such as dx (diagnosis), and $rads$ (radiation, radiotherapy). Thus, they may be reflective of identification with a broader community of cancer patients who are internet users. Other often used abbreviations are dh (dear husband), dd (dear daughter), etc. We also observed that users frequently refer to members of the community by name and even as $sister(s)$.

Now let us look at some examples illustrating these patterns of language change. We take as an example a specific long-time user. We start with a post from early in her participation, specifically from a couple of days after her registration:

I am also new to the forum, but not new to bc, diagnosed last yr, [..] My follow-up with surgeon for reports is not until 8/9 over a week later. My husband too is so wonderful, only married a yr in May, 1 month before bc diagnosed, I could not get through this if it weren't for him, never misses an appointment, [...] I wish everyone well. We will all survive.

The next two posts[1] are from the same user, 2 to 4 years after her registration date. Both posts are directed to other forum members, very informal, and contain a lot of abbreviations (e.g. '*DH*' (Dear Husband), '*DD*' (Dear Daughter), '*SIL*' (Son in Law)).

Gee Ann I think we may have shared the same 'moment in time' boy I am getting paid back big time for my fun in the sun. Well Rose enjoy your last day of freedom - LOL. Have lots of fun with DH 'The Harley'. Ride long and hard (either one you choose - OOPS).

Oh Kim- sorry you have so much going on - and an idiot DH on top of it all. [..] Steph- vent away - that sucks - [..] XOXOXOXOXOXOXOX [..], quiet weekend kids went to DD's & SIL on Friday evening, they take them to school [..], made an AM pop in as I am supposed to, SIL is an idiot but then you all know that.

This anecdotal evidence illustrates the linguistic shift we will now provide quantitative evidence for.

4 Patterns of language change

4.1 Approach

In this section we aggregate data across long time participants and look at global patterns of language change. Specifically, we will analyze patterns of change in the first year after registration of these members, and show how language patterns consistently become more different from the first week of participation and more similar to the stable pattern found within the second year of data. Furthermore, when comparing consecutive weeks we find that the difference increases and then stabilizes by the end of the first year. The unit of analysis is one week of data. Because there are multiple ways to measure the similarity or difference between two distributions, we explore the use of two different methods. The first metric we use is the Kullback-Leibler (KL) divergence. Larger values indicate bigger differences in distribution. P represents the true distribution. Note that this metric is asymmetric.

$$KL(P,Q) = \sum_i P(i) \log \frac{P(i)}{Q(i)}$$

We also explore using the Spearman's Rank Correlation Coefficient (SRCC), which measures the similarity of two rankings:

$$SRCC = 1 - \frac{6 \sum_i d_i^2}{n(n^2-1)}$$

Where d_i is the difference between the ranks of word i in the two rankings and n is the total number of words.

4.2 Sampling

In this analysis, we begin by aligning the data of every member by registration date. We then aggregate posts of all users by week. Thus, in week 1, we have the posts from all users during the first week after their registration. Note that the actual week in time would not be the same for each of these users since they did not all register at the same time. In this way, a week worth of data represents the way users talk after the corresponding number of weeks after registering with the community rather than representing a specific period of time. Because our dataset spans a large time period of time (i.e. more than 8 years), it is very unlikely that patterns we find in the data reflect external events from any specific time period.

As discussed before, a large proportion of members only post in their first week after registration. These short time members might already initially differ from members who tend to participate longer in the forum. Therefore, it might confuse the model if we take these short time members into account. We may observe apparent changes in language that are artifacts of the difference in distribution of users across weeks. Thus, because we are interested in language change specifically, we only consider posts of long-term participants.

[1]Names are replaced in example

In addition, we have limited our focus to the initial two-year period of participation, because it is for this length of participation that we have enough users and enough posts to make a computational model feasible. We have also limited ourselves to examining high frequency words, because we have a large vocabulary but only a limited amount of data per week. Two weeks can look artificially similar if they both have a lot of non-occurring words. In summary, taking above considerations into account, we applied the following procedure:

- We only look at the first 2 years, for which we still have a large amount of data for every week.
- We only look at members who are long-term participants (2 years or longer), this leaves us with 3,012 users.
- For every week, we randomly sample an equal number of posts (i.e., 600 from each week). All posts are taken into account (i.e. both responses as well as thread openings).
- We only look at the distribution change of high frequency words (words occurring at least 1,000 times), this leaves us with 1,540 unique words. No stemming or stop word removal was done.

Figure 1: KL divergence between weeks in first year and overall second year.

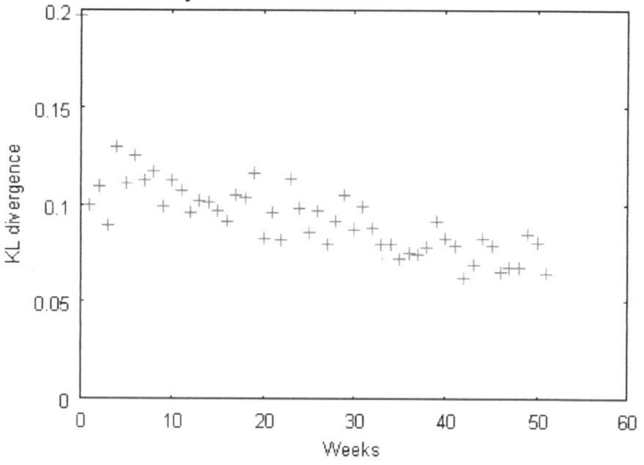

Figure 2: KL divergence between weeks in first year and first week.

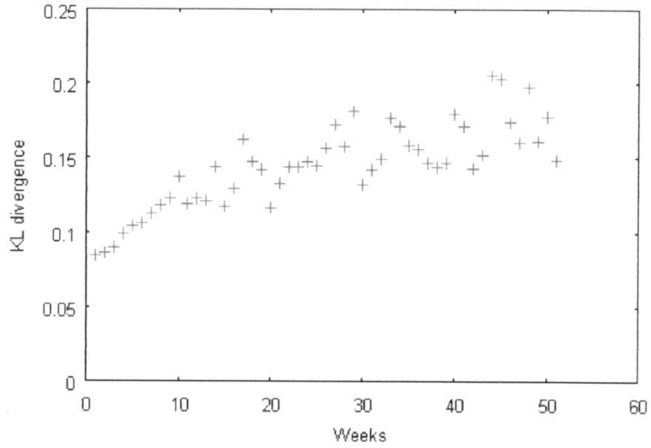

4.3 Comparison with early and late distributions

Using the dataset described in the previous section, we compare the language of each week during the first year after registration with language in the very first week and with language in the second year.

First we analyze whether language in the first year becomes more similar to language used by members in their second year as time progresses. We therefore compare the word distributions of the weeks of the first year with the overall word distribution of the second year. We apply KL divergence where we consider the distribution of the second year as the 'true distribution'. The result is shown in Figure 1. We see that the KL divergence decreases, which means that as time progresses, the word distributions look more like the distribution of the second year. Fitting a Least Squares (LS) model, we get an intercept of 0.121033 and slope of -0.001080 ($r^2 = 0.5528$). Using the Spearman Rank Correlation (SRCC) and fitting a LS model, we observe the same pattern ($r^2 = 0.6435$).

Our second analysis involves comparing the distributions of the first year (excluding the first week), with the distribution of the first week. The result is shown in Figure 2. We see that the KL divergence increases, meaning that as time progresses, the word distributions become less similar with the first week. (KL: $r^2 = 0.6643$, SRCC: $r^2 = 0.7962$).

4.4 Comparing consecutive distributions

We now compare the distributions of consecutive weeks to see how much language change occurs in different time periods. For KL divergence we use the symmetric version. Results are presented in Figure 3 and show a divergence pattern throughout the first year that stabilizes towards the end of that first year of participation. (KL: $r^2 = 0.4726$, SRCC: $r^2 =$

Figure 3: KL divergence between consecutive weeks.

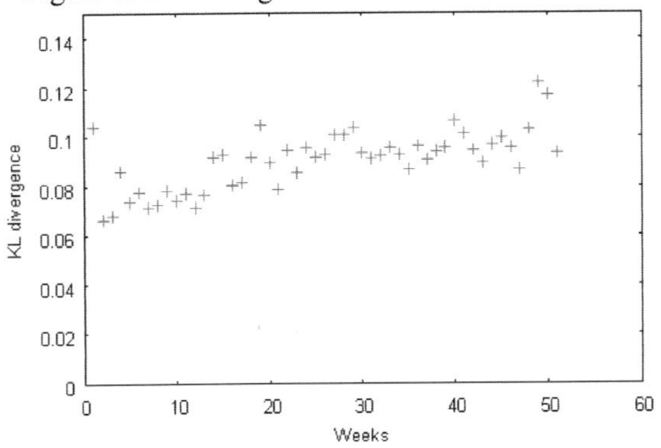

0.8178). The divergence pattern was also observed by Huffaker et al. (2006) (related, but not equivalent setting, as mentioned in the literature review). We hypothesize that the divergence occurs because users tend to talk about a progressively broader set of topics as they become more involved in the community. To confirm this hypothesis, we compare the distributions of each week with the uniform distribution. We indeed find that as time progresses, the distributions for each week become more uniform. (KL: $r^2 = 0.3283$, SRCC: $r^2 = 0.6435$).

5 Predicting membership duration

In the previous section we found strong patterns of language change in our data. We are interested in the extent to which we can automatically predict *how many weeks* the user has been a member, using only text or meta-features from that specific week. Identifying which features predict how long a member has been active can give more detailed insight into the social language that characterizes the community. In addition, it tells us how prominent the pattern is among other sources of language variation.

5.1 Dataset

For this analysis, we set up the data slightly differently. Now, rather than combine data across users, we keep the data from each user for each week separate so we can make a separate prediction for each user during each week of their participation. Thus, for each person, we aggregate all posts per week. We only consider weeks in the first two years after the registration in which there were at least 10 posts with at least 10 tokens from that user.

Table 2: Statistics dataset.

	#Docs	#Persons	#Posts
Training	13,273	1,591	380,143
Development	4,617	548	122,489
Test	4,571	548	134,141

5.2 Approach

Given an input vector $\mathbf{x} \in \mathbb{R}^m$ containing the features, we aim to find a prediction $\hat{y} \in \mathbb{R}$ for the number of weeks the person has been a member of the community $y \in \mathbb{R}$ using a linear regression model: $\hat{y} = \beta_0 + \mathbf{x}^\top \boldsymbol{\beta}$ where β_0 and $\boldsymbol{\beta}$ are the parameters to estimate. Usually, the parameters are learned by minimizing the sum of squared errors.

In order to strive for a model with high explanatory value, we use Linear Regression, with L1 regularization (Tibshirani, 1996). This minimizes the sum of squared errors, but in addition adds a penalty term $\lambda \sum_{j=1}^{m} |\beta_j|$, the sum of absolute values of the coefficients. λ is a constant and can be found by optimizing over the development data. As a result, this method delivers sparse models. We use Orthant-Wise Limited-memory Quasi-Newton Optimizer (Andrew and Gao, 2007) as our optimization method. This method has proven to establish competitive performances with other optimization methods, while producing sparse models (Gao et al., 2007).

Because our observations suggest that language change decreases as members have been active longer, we also experimented with applying a log transformation on the number of weeks.

5.3 Features

For all features, we only use information that has been available for that particular week. We explore different types of features related to the qualitative differences in language we discussed in Section 3: textual, behavioral, subforum and meta-features.

5.3.1 Textual features

We explore the following textual features:

- *Unigrams* and *bigrams*.
- *Part of Speech* (POS) bigrams. Text was tagged using the Stanford POS tagger (Toutanova et al., 2003).

- *LIWC* (Pennebaker et al., 2001), a word counting program that captures word classes and stylistic features.

- *Usernames*. Because some of the usernames are common words, we only consider usernames of users active in the same thread.

- *Proper names*. We obtained a list containing common female names. We ranked them according to frequency in our dataset, and manually deleted common words in our dataset, such as *happy, hope, tuesday* and *may*, from our list.

- *Slang words*. We manually compile a list of common abbreviations and their whole words counterpart. We then count the number of abbreviations and the number of whole words used in the post. The feature value then is $(\#abbrev - \#wholewords)/\#totalwords$. Because in some contexts no abbreviations can be used, this feature takes into account if the user actually chose to use the abbreviation/whole word, or if there was no need for it.

No stemming or stopword removal is used. Frequencies are normalized by length.

5.3.2 Behavioral features

We also explore additional features that indicate the behavior of the user:

- Ratio (posts starting threads) / (total number of posts).

- Number of posts.

5.3.3 Subforum features

We include as features the distribution of subforums the member has posted in. This captures two intuitions. First, it is an approximation of the current phase in the cancer process for that member. For example, we noticed that most of the new users have just been diagnosed, while long term users have already finished treatment. Because the subforums are very specific (such as '*Not Diagnosed with a Recurrence or Metastases but Concerned*'), we expect these features to give a good approximation of the phase the user is currently in. In addition, these subforums also give an indication of the user's interest. For example, whether the user posts mostly in medical forums, or mostly in the social orientated subforums.

Table 3: Results reported with Pearsons correlation (r).

Run	# Features	Raw (r)	Log (r)
Unigrams + Bigrams	43,126	0.547	0.621
POS	1,258	0.409	0.437
LIWC	88	0.494	0.492
Proper names	1	0.185	0.186
Usernames	1	0.150	0.102
Slang	1	0.092	0.176
Behavior	2	0.139	0.243
Subforum	65	0.404	0.419
All above	44,542	0.581	0.649
All above + Person	46,133	0.586	0.656

5.3.4 Other features

Most of the persons appear multiple times in our dataset (e.g. multiple weeks). To help the model control for idiosyncratic features of individual users, we include for every person a dummy variable associated with that user's unique identity. This helps the model at training time to separate variance in language usage across users from general effects related to length of participation. Note that we do not use these features as test time.

5.4 Results

We experimented with individual types of features as well as all of them aggregated. The results (correlations) can be found in Table 3. The features having the most weight for long time participants in our best model (All incl. Person, Log) are presented in Table 4. We see that for most features the performance was higher when applying the log transformation. This was especially the case with the unigrams and bigrams features. For some features the difference was less, such as for proper names and the subforum features. This could indicate that these features have a more linear pattern as time progresses, while word patterns such as unigrams tend to stabilize earlier. We find that both stylistic patterns (such as POS) as well as patterns indicating conformity (social behavior, slang words) are individually already very predictive.

In our best performing model, we find that both

Table 5: Qualitative grouping of textual features.

Type	Short time members	Long time members
Abbreviations	Husband	My DD (Dear Daughter), Your PS (Plastic Surgeon)
Social networks		Facebook, fb
Greetings	Hi all	Hi girls, Hi gals
I versus other	LIWC-I, My, Me	LIWC-other, We, Sisters
Social support		Hugs, Condolences, So sorry
Thanking	Thanks, Thanx, Thx	
Forum		Bc org, On bco
Introducing	Newbie, New here, Am new	
Asking information	Info, LIWC-qmarks	

Table 4: Top 10 features of long term users.

Feature	Weight
META - slang	0.058362195
META -propername	0.052984915
year	0.050872918
META - [person1]	0.050708718
META - [person2]	0.040548104
months	0.040400583
META - [person3]	0.039806096
LIWC - Othref	0.036080545
META - [person4]	0.035605996
POS - nnp prp	0.035033650

the slang and proper name features get a high weight for long time participants. Furthermore, we observe that a lot of the person meta features are included in the model when it is trained, although as mentioned we do not use these features at testing time. The fact that the model assigns them weight indicates that idiosyncratic features of users explain a lot of variance in the data. Our best performing model has 3,518 non zero features. In Table 5 we qualitatively grouped and contrasted features that were more associated with short-term or long-term members. We see that long-term members show much more social behavior and familiarity with each other. This is shown to references to each other, more social support, references to social networks and ways of greeting. They furthermore talk about the forum itself more often by using the abbreviation *'bco'*. Short term members are characterized by words that are used when they introduce themselves to others.

Thus we find that long time participants are characterized by informal language, containing many forum specific jargon, as well as showing emotional involvement with other forum members. Our best run obtained a correlation of $r = 0.656$, giving an r^2 value of 0.430. This means that 0.43 of the variation can be explained by our model. Since there are many other factors that influence the writing of users, it is understandable that our model does not explain all the variance.

6 Discussion

As discussed widely in previous literature, people become socialized into communities over time through their interactions with community members. The extent of conformity to group norms reflects commitment to the group. Our first study showed evidence of increasing conformity to community norms through changes in simple word distributions. The second study then tested the robustness of these findings through a prediction task and extended the language features of the first study.

Since community members tend to conform increasingly to community norms over time, although the target class for our predictive model is time, it is reasonable to assume that what the model really learns to predict is how long average community members have been around by the time they sound like that. In other words, one can think about its time prediction as a measure of how long it sounds like that person has been in the community. The model would therefore overpredict for members who move from the periphery to the core of a community faster than average while underpredicting for those who do so more gradually. This would be consistent with the idea that rate of commitment making and conformity is person specific.

There are two limitations that need to be addressed regarding the present studies. First, there are certain factors that influence the rate of adoption to the forum that we are not able to take into account. For example, some people might have already been reading the forum for a while, before they actually decide to join the community. These people are already exposed to the community practices, and therefore might already show more conformity in the beginning than others.

Second, our experiments involved one online community targeting a very specific topic. Due to the nature of the topic, most of the active users come from a small subpopulation (mostly women between 40-60 years). Therefore, it is a question how well these results can be applied to other online communities.

As a future application, a model that can capture these changes could be used in research related to commitment in online communities.

7 Conclusion

It is widely accepted that persistent language change in individuals occurs over time as a result of the accumulation of local processes of accommodation. Although previous research has looked at accommodation within short periods of time, including recent research on social media data, persistent language change as a result of longer term involvement in an online community is still an understudied area.

In this paper we have presented research aiming to close this gap. We have analyzed data from a large online breast cancer forum. Analyzing data of long time members, we found strong patterns indicating language changes as these members participated in the community, especially over the course of their first year of participation.

We then presented a regression approach to predict how long a person has been a member of the community. Long time participants were characterized by showing more social behavior. Furthermore, they used more forum specific language, such as certain abbreviations and ways of greeting. Due to the nature of our dataset, language was also influenced by external factors such as changes in the cancer process of individuals.

Although our observations are intuitive and agree with observations in previous, related literature regarding socialization in communities, it is still a question whether our observations generalize to other online communities.

In our current work we have looked at changes across users and across contexts. However, it is well known that individuals adapt their language depending on local interactions. Thus, a next step would be to model the process by which local accommodation accumulates and results in long term language change.

Acknowledgments

The authors would like to thank Michael Heilman for the regression code and Noah Smith for ideas for the regression experiments. This work was funded by NSF grant IIS-0968485.

References

Galen Andrew and Jianfeng Gao. 2007. Scalable training of l1-regularized log-linear models. In *Proceedings of the 24th international conference on Machine learning*, ICML '07, pages 33–40, New York, NY, USA. ACM.

Justine Cassell and Dona Tversky. 2005. The language of online intercultural community formation. *Journal of Computer-Mediated Communication*, 10:16–33.

Cristian Danescu-Niculescu-Mizil, Michael Gamon, and Susan Dumais. 2011. Mark my words! linguistic style accommodation in social media. In *Proceedings of WWW*.

Penelope Eckert and John R. Rickford. 2001. *Style and Sociolinguistic Variation*. Cambridge: University of Cambridge Press.

Jianfeng Gao, Galen Andrew, Mark Johnson, and Kristina Toutanova. 2007. A comparative study of parameter estimation methods for statistical natural language processing. In *Proceedings of the 45th Annual Meeting of the Association of Computational Linguistics*, pages 824–831, Prague, Czech Republic, June. Association for Computational Linguistics.

Howard Giles, Donald M. Taylor, and Richard Bourhis. 1973. Towards a theory of interpersonal accommodation through language: some canadian data. *Language in Society*, 2(02):177–192.

Amy L. Gonzales, Jeffrey T. Hancock, and James W. Pennebaker. 2010. Language style matching as a predictor of social dynamics in small groups. *Communication Research*, 37(1):3–19, February.

David Huffaker, Joseph Jorgensen, Francisco Iacobelli, Paul Tepper, and Justine Cassell. 2006. Computational measures for language similarity across time in online communities. In *Proceedings of the HLT-NAACL 2006 Workshop on Analyzing Conversations in Text and Speech*, ACTS, pages 15–22, Stroudsburg, PA, USA. Association for Computational Linguistics.

Mukund Jha and Noémie Elhadad. 2010. Cancer stage prediction based on patient online discourse. In *Proceedings of the 2010 Workshop on Biomedical Natural Language Processing*, BioNLP '10, pages 64–71, Stroudsburg, PA, USA. Association for Computational Linguistics.

William Labov. 2010a. *Principles of Linguistic Change, Volume I, Internal Factors*. Wiley-Blackwell.

William Labov. 2010b. *Principles of Linguistic Change, Volume I, Social Factors*. Wiley-Blackwell.

Wan S. E. Lam. 2008. Language socialization in online communities. In Nancy H. Hornberger, editor, *Encyclopedia of Language and Education*, pages 2859–2869. Springer US.

Jean Lave and Etienne Wenger. 1991. *Situated Learning. Legitimate peripheral participation*. Cambridge: University of Cambridge Press.

Dong Nguyen, Elijah Mayfield, and Carolyn P. Rose. 2010. An analysis of perspectives in interactive settings. In *Proceedings of the 2010 KDD Workshop on Social Media Analytics*.

Kate G. Niederhoffer and James W. Pennebaker. 2002. Linguistic style matching in social interaction.

John C. Paolillo. 2001. Language variation on internet relay chat: A social network approach. *Journal of Sociolinguistics*, 5:180–213.

James W. Pennebaker, Roger J. Booth, and Martha E. Francis, 2001. *Linguistic Inquiry and Word Count (LIWC): A Computerized Text Analysis Program*.

Tom Postmes, Russell Spears, and Martin Lea. 2000. The formation of group norms in computer-mediated communication. *Human Communication Research*, 26(3):341–371.

Lauren E. Scissors, Alastair J. Gill, Kathleen Geraghty, and Darren Gergle. 2009. In cmc we trust: the role of similarity. In *Proceedings of the 27th international conference on Human factors in computing systems*, CHI '09, pages 527–536, New York, NY, USA. ACM.

Robert Tibshirani. 1996. Regression shrinkage and selection via the lasso. *Journal of the Royal Statistical Society. Series B (Methodological)*, 58(1):267–288.

Kristina Toutanova, Dan Klein, Christopher D. Manning, and Yoram Singer. 2003. Feature-rich part-of-speech tagging with a cyclic dependency network. In *Proceedings of the 2003 Conference of the North American Chapter of the Association for Computational Linguistics on Human Language Technology - Volume 1*, NAACL '03, pages 173–180, Stroudsburg, PA, USA. Association for Computational Linguistics.

Email Formality in the Workplace: A Case Study on the Enron Corpus

Kelly Peterson, Matt Hohensee, and Fei Xia
Linguistics Department
University of Washington
Seattle, WA 98195
{kellypet, hohensee, fxia}@uw.edu

Abstract

Email is an important way of communication in our daily life and it has become the subject of various NLP and social studies. In this paper, we focus on email formality and explore the factors that could affect the sender's choice of formality. As a case study, we use the Enron email corpus to test how formality is affected by social distance, relative power, and the weight of imposition, as defined in Brown and Levinson's model of politeness (1987). Our experiments show that their model largely holds in the Enron corpus. We believe that the methodology proposed in the paper can be applied to other social media domains and be used to test other linguistic or social theories.

1 Introduction

Email has become an important way of communication in our daily life. Because of its wide usage, it has been the subject of various studies such as social network analysis (e.g., (Leuski, 2004; Diesner et al., 2005; Carvalho et al., 2007)), deception detection (e.g., (Zhou et al., 2004; Keila and Skillcorn, 2005)), information extraction (e.g., (Culotta et al., 2004; Minkov et al., 2005)), and topic discovery (e.g., (McCallum et al., 2007)). In this study, we focus on email formality in various social settings; that is, we want to determine whether the choice of formality in email communication is affected by factors such as the social distance and relative power between the senders and the recipients.

While an early perspective of email communication held that email is a lean medium which lacks vital social cues (Daft and Lengel, 1986), other work has shown that senders of email exhibit a wide range of language and form choices which vary in different social contexts (Orlikowski and Yates, 1994). Through various theories of sociolinguistics, it is proposed that these changes take place in a predictable manner.

Brown and Levinson (1987) have proposed a model where in order to save the "face" or public self image of the hearer of a message, a speaker can employ a range of verbal strategies. Their model of politeness states that in social situations there are three factors which are considered in a decision whether or when to use communication techniques such as formality:

1. The "social distance" between the participants as a symmetric relation
2. The relative "power" between the participants as an asymmetric relation
3. The weight of an imposition such as a request

Abdullah (2006) examines email interactions from the perspective of Brown and Levinson's politeness model in a Malaysian corporation from over 180 participants and a corpus of 770 email messages. This work directly examines the factors mentioned previously which influence email formality. Unfortunately, the methodology and data were not provided for this study.

The goal of our work is to test whether Brown and Levinson's model holds in a real setting with a much larger data set. In this study, we chose the Enron Email Corpus as our dataset. We first built two classifiers: one labels an email as *formal* or *informal* and the other determines whether an email contains a request. Next, we used the classifiers to label every email in the Enron corpus. Finally, we tested whether the three factors in Brown and Levinson's theory indeed affect formality in email communication. While we consider the work a case study, we believe that the methodology proposed in the paper can be applied to other social media domains and be used to test other linguistic or social theories.[1]

2 Overview of the Enron email corpus

The Enron email corpus, which consists of hundreds of thousands of emails from over a hundred Enron employees over a period of 3.5 years (1998 to 2002), was made public during the US government's legal investigation of Enron. The corpus was first processed and released by Klimt and Yang (2004) at Carnegie Mellon University (CMU), and this CMU dataset has later been re-processed by several other research groups. In this section, we briefly introduce the datasets that we used in our experiments.

2.1 The ISI dataset

The CMU dataset contains many duplicates. It was later processed and cleaned by Shetty and Adibi at ISI and released as a relational database. The ISI database comprises 252,759 messages from the email folders of 150 employees (Shetty and Adibi, 2004).[2] We use the ISI dataset as the starting point for all of our experiments except for the one in Section 5.1.

2.2 The Sheffield dataset

The Enron email corpus contains both personal and business emails. In 2006, Jabbari and his colleagues at the University of Sheffield manually annotated a subset of the emails in the CMU dataset with "Business" or "Personal" categories (Jabbari et al., 2006). The subset contains 14,818 emails and 3,598 of them (24.2%) are labeled as "personal".[3] We use this dataset in the personal vs. business experiment as described in Section 5.1.[4]

2.3 The ISI Enron employee position table

In addition to the ISI database, ISI also provided a table of 161 employees and their positions in the company.[5] In Section 5.3, we study the effect of seniority on the formality of a message, and we use this table to determine the relative seniority between senders and recipients of a given email.

3 Creating the gold standard

In this study, we build two classifiers: a formality classifier that determines whether an email is formal, and a request classifier that determines whether an email contains a request. In order to train and evaluate the classifiers, 400 email messages were randomly chosen from the Enron corpus and manually labeled for formality and request.

3.1 Formality annotation

Formality is a concept which is difficult to define precisely and human judgment on whether an email is formal can be subjective. To determine how much human annotators can agree on the concept, we asked three annotators to label 100 out of the 400 emails with four labels: "very formal", "somewhat formal", "somewhat informal", and "very informal".

Because formality is hard to define, we did not give annotators a concrete definition. Instead, we provided a few guidelines and asked annotators to follow the guidelines and their intuition. One of these guidelines was that the formality of an email should not necessarily be dictated by the relationship between the sender and the recipient if their relationship can be inferred from the message. Another guideline stressed that the nature of an email being business or personal should not necessarily dictate its formality. Other than these guidelines, annotators were asked to come up with their own criteria for formality while doing the annotation.

Table 1 shows the agreement between each annotator pair and the average score of the three pairs. For agreement, we calculated the accuracy, which

[1] Our data including annotations and results can be found at http://students.washington.edu/kellypet/enron-formality/

[2] The dataset can be downloaded from http://www.isi.edu/~adibi/Enron/Enron.htm

[3] The dataset is available at http://staffwww.dcs.shef.ac.uk/people/L.Guthrie/nlp/research.htm.

[4] The ISI dataset and the Sheffield dataset contain significant overlap as both were derived from the CMU dataset, but the former is not necessarily a superset of the latter.

[5] We downloaded the table in January 2011 from http://www.isi.edu/~adibi/Enron/Enron_Employee_Status.xls

Annotator pair	2-way Agreement (Acc/F1)	4-way Agreement (Acc)
A vs. B	87.3/77.8	53.7
A vs. C	85.4/77.2	40.6
B vs. C	84.5/72.9	36.1
Pairwise Ave	85.7/76.0	43.5

Table 1: Inter-annotator agreement for formality annotation

is the percentage of emails that receive the same label from the two annotators. *2-way agreement* means the agreement is calculated after the label *very formal* has been merged with *somewhat formal*, and *very informal* with *somewhat informal*; *4-way agreement* means that the agreement is calculated with the four formality labels used by the annotators. With the 2-way distinction (formal vs. informal), we also calculate the f-score for identifying *informal* emails, treating one annotation as the gold standard and the other as the system output. This table shows that, although the concept of formality is intuitive, the inter-annotator agreement on formality is pretty low (especially when making the 4-way distinction).

Finally, Annotator A, who had the highest agreement with other annotators, annotated the remaining 300 emails, and his annotation was treated as the gold standard for our formality classifier.

3.2 Request annotation

In order to train and evaluate our request classifier, we asked two annotators to go over the same 400 emails and label each message as *containing-request* or *no-request*. A message is considered to contain a request if it is clear that the sender of the message expects the recipient to take some action to respond to the message. For instance, if a message includes a question such as *what do you think?* or a request such as *please call me tomorrow*, it should be labeled as *containing-request* as the sender expects the recipient to call the sender or answer the question. Our definition is slightly different from the definition of *request* used in speech acts, and it can be seen as a synonym of *require-action*.

While some emails clearly contain requests and others clearly do not, there is some gray area in between, which results in the disagreement between the annotators. Many of the disagreed emails include sentences such as *Let me know if you have any questions*. This very commonly used expression is itself ambiguous between the meanings *"Let me know whether you have any questions"* and *"If you have any questions, please inform me of that fact"*. Furthermore, this sentence often appears as a marker of politeness or an offer to clarify further, rather than a request for action. So the correct label of an email containing this expression depends on the context. For the 400 messages, the two annotators agreed on 361 messages, for an inter-annotator agreement of 90.3% and a F1-score of 87.9% for identifying emails that contain requests.

4 Building classifiers

In this section, we discuss the feature sets used for the two classifiers and report their performances.

4.1 Data pre-processing

Before forming the feature vectors for the classifiers, we preprocessed all the emails in the ISI and Sheffield dataset in several steps. First, we removed any replied or forwarded message from the email body as we want to use only the text written by the sender. If the email body becomes empty after this step, the email is excluded from the analysis conducted in Section 5. After this step, the size of the ISI dataset reduces from 252,759 to 232,815 emails, and the size of the Sheffield dataset changes from 14,818 to 13,882 emails. Second, the email messages were segmented into sentences and tokenized with tools in the NLTK package (Bird et al., 2009).

4.2 Formality classifier

For the formality classifier, we use two labels: *formal* and *informal*.

4.2.1 Features for formality

During formality annotation, after the 100 emails had been annotated, the three annotators were asked to provide a few paragraphs describing their criteria for formality. In these criteria, more cues are indicators of informality (e.g., the use of vulgar words) than indicators of formality. We use the following features to capture the informal "style" of the emails:[6]

F1: Informal Word Features, which check the occurrences of *informal words* (see the next section for detail)

F2: Punctuation Features:

- Exclamation Points ('!')
- Absence of sentence final punctuation
- Frequency of ellipsis ('...')

F3: Case features:

- All lowercase Subject line
- Frequency of sentences which were entirely lower case
- Frequency of sentences whose first word is lower case

4.2.2 Informal words

We designed a simple heuristic method to extract a list of informal words from the Enron corpus. First, we collect all the unigrams in the Enron corpus. Second, we retrieve the information about each unigram from Wordnik,[7] a website that provides access to retrieve word definitions from multiple source dictionaries. Among the several dictionaries crawled by Wordnik, we find Wiktionary to be the best source for our task since its labels on word definitions such as 'informal', 'offensive', 'vulgar', 'colloquial' and 'misspelling' were the most consistent and relevant to our definition of "formality". In addition to these labels, the part of speech category for 'interjection' was also used to determine if a word might be considered informal in email communication. Third, we use the gathered word definitions to determine whether a word is *informal*.

One issue with the last step is that words often have multiple meanings and some meanings are informal and others are not. For instance, the word *bloody* can be formal or informal depending on which meaning is used in an email. As word sense disambiguation is out of the scope of this work, we use some simple heuristics to determine whether a word should be treated as informal or not. In essence, the process treats a word as informal if a large percentage of definitions for the word have certain labels (e.g., *vulgar*, *offensive*, and *misspelling*) or certain part-of-speech tags (e.g., *interjection*).[8]

4.2.3 Performance of the formality classifier

We trained a Maximum Entropy (MaxEnt) classifier in the Mallet package (McCallum, 2002). Table 2 shows classification accuracy and precision, recall, and F1-score for identifying informal emails. The baseline system labels every email as *formal* because 62.7% of the emails in the dataset were annotated as formal; its F1-score is zero as the recall is zero. The numbers for the inter-annotator agreement row are copied from the pairwise average of the 2-way agreement in Table 1. The table shows that, with very few features, the performance of the formality classifier is much better than the baseline and is close to inter-annotator agreement. All three types of features beat the baselines and combining them provides additional improvement.

	Acc	Prec	Rec	F1
Baseline	62.7	-	-	-
Inter-annotator agreement	85.7	89.5	66.8	76.0
F1: Informal words	69.2	75.0	26.7	39.3
F2: Punctuation	74.4	82.5	45.8	58.9
F3: Case features	69.7	80.0	26.5	39.8
F1+F2	76.4	77.3	51.1	61.5
F1+F3	72.8	74.3	39.4	51.5
F2+F3	80.3	85.2	59.7	70.2
F1+F2+F3	80.6	85.7	62.1	72.0

Table 2: Performance of the formality classifier. We use 10-fold cross validation on the 400 emails. Baseline: label every email as *formal*.

4.3 Request classifier

The request classifier uses two labels: *containing-request* and *no-request*.

[6]We did not use ngram features as they might be too specific to the small training data we have and might not work well when applied to other emails in the Enron corpus or emails in other domain.

[7]http://www.wordnik.com

[8]We manually checked the list of informal words extracted and estimated that the number the false positives is less than 1%. However, the list is definitely not complete as many informal words in the Enron corpus do not appear in the dictionaries used by Wordnik.

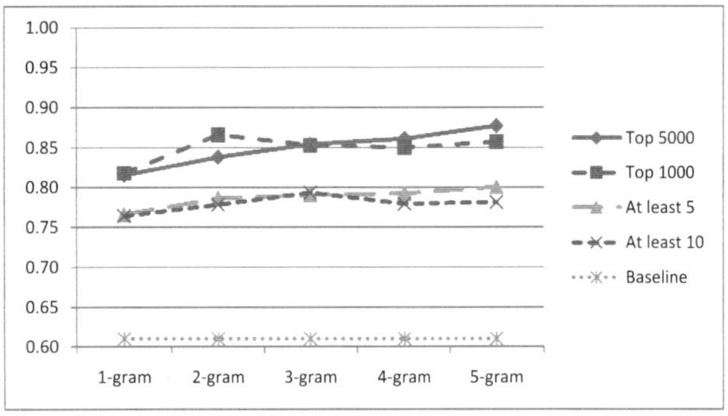

Figure 1: Accuracy of the request classifier with different feature sets

4.3.1 Features for request

There has been considerable research into categorizing email messages by function. Cohen, Carvalho, and Mitchell (2004) described the classification of email into 'email speech acts', building on the speech act theory of Searle (1975). Carvalho and Cohen (2006) achieved high-precision results categorizing messages into categories such as 'request' and 'proposal' when preprocessing the text in certain ways and using unigram, bigram, and trigram features only.

Unlike formality, which is more about the style of the messages (e.g., whether the email is all in lowercase), the content words are more relevant for identifying requests. Following the work in (Carvalho and Cohen, 2006), we used word ngrams as features. To prevent the features from being too specific to the small training data, we experimented with two ways of feature selection: by feature counts and by chi-square scores. N-grams were extracted from the email body only. For pre-processing, in addition to the pre-processing step mentioned in 4.1, we also replaced some name entities (e.g., numbers and dates) with special labels and lowercased the text.

4.3.2 Performance of the request classifier

We trained a MaxEnt classifier and ran 10-fold cross validation on the 400-email dataset. Figure 1 shows the accuracy of the classifier with different feature sets. The bottom dotted line is the baseline result. In the 400 emails, 244 are labeled as *no-request*, so a baseline system that labels everything as *no-request* has an accuracy of 61%. The middle two lines are the accuracy with features that occur no fewer than 5 or 10 times. For the top two curves, features are sorted according to the chi-square scores, and the top one thousand or five thousand are kept. X-axis shows the value of n for word ngrams; e.g., 3-gram means features include word unigrams, bigrams, and trigrams. Figure 1 shows that chi-square scores outperform feature counts for feature selection, and varying the value of n does not affect the accuracy very much.

Table 3 shows classification accuracy and precision, recall, and F1-score for identifying request-containing emails when n is set to 3. The table shows that our classifier, regardless of methods used for feature selection, greatly outperforms the baseline system, and there is a small gap between the performance of our classifier and the inter-annotator agreement. For the rest of our experiment, we will use 3-gram, Top5000 as the feature set for the request classifier.

	Acc	Prec	Rec	F1
Baseline	61.0	-	-	-
Inter-annotator agreement	90.3	90.4	85.5	87.9
Using all features	79.5	76.8	68.0	72.1
At least 5	79.0	75.7	68.0	71.6
At least 10	79.3	75.9	68.6	72.1
Top1000	85.5	88.3	72.4	79.6
Top5000	85.5	88.3	72.4	79.6

Table 3: Performance of the request classifier with 3-gram features: We use 10-fold cross validation on the 400 emails. Baseline: label every email as *no-request*.

5 Factors influencing formality

As mentioned in Section 1, Brown and Levinson (1987) proposed three factors that influence communication choices such as formality: social distance, relative power, and the weight of an imposition. In this section, we test whether these factors indeed affect formality in emails.

We measure social distance in two ways: one is based on the nature of emails (personal vs. business), and the other is based on the number of emails sent from the sender to the recipient. While these aspects do not directly define the social distance between individuals, they are employed to illustrate related social properties in absence of data which outlines the social distance of all Enron employees. For relative power, we use the rank difference of the positions that the sender and the recipient held in Enron. Since relative power is complex to define without more data, this definition of rank difference serves as one dimension in which we can study relative power. For the weight of imposition, we compare emails that contain requests and the ones that do not.

5.1 Social distance: Personal vs. Business

In general, friends, family and other such personal contacts are presumably closer in social distance than business colleagues. Therefore, it is possible that email messages of a personal nature will be more likely to be informal than those of a business nature. To test the hypothesis, we compare the degree of formality in business vs. personal emails. We use the Sheffield dataset, which contains 13,822 non-empty emails that have been manually labeled as "personal" or "business". We ran the formality classifier on the data, and the results are in Table 4. The first and second columns show the number of emails that are labeled as *formal* or *informal* by our formality classifier, and the last column shows the percentage of emails in that row that are labeled *informal* (a.k.a. *the rate of informality*).

The table demonstrates that the rate of informality in personal emails (56.0%) is indeed much higher than that of business emails (21.3%). We have run the Chi-square test and G test with the counts in the table, and both tests indicate that formality (formal vs. informal) is not independent from the business nature of an email message (business vs. personal) at p=0.0001. The same is true for formality and other social factors that we tested in this section (see Tables 5, 7, 8, and 9).[9]

[9]There are two caveats for using these statistical tests to determine whether two random variables (formality and a social factor) are independent. First, the counts in the tables are based on the output of the two classifiers, which could be different from the real counts. Second, the data points in some experiments were not chosen randomly from the whole email corpus; for instance, the emails in Table 7 were from a small set of people whose ranks at Enron were known.

	Formal	Informal	Inf %
Personal	1410	1793	56.0%
Business	8409	2270	21.3%
Total	9819	4063	29.3%

Table 4: Formality in personal vs business emails, $p < 0.0001$

5.2 Social distance: Amount of contact

Besides the difference in personal and business matters, another way to measure social distance is the amount of contact that two individuals have with each other. People with more email exchange are likely to be closer in social distance than those with less email exchange, and are therefore likely to have a higher rate of informality. To test this hypothesis, we started with the ISI dataset and looked at the subset of emails where an email has exactly one recipient, and both the sender and the recipient are in the enron.com domain. The emails were then grouped into several buckets based on the number of emails from a sender to a recipient.

The results are in Table 5. The first column is the range of the numbers of emails from a sender to a recipient, and the last column is the number of (sender, recipient) pairs where the number of emails that the sender sent to the recipient is in the range specified in the first column. The second column is the total number of *formal* emails from the senders to the recipients in those pairs. The third column is defined similarly, and the 4th column is the rate of informality. Note that the rates of informality in the first two rows are about the same; it might be due to the fact that the Enron corpus contains emails only in a 3.5-year period. The rate of formality does go up in the third and fourth rows.

Emails sent from A to B	Formal	Inf	Inf %	# of pairs
1 to 10	23,423	7,566	24.4%	14,877
11 to 50	11,484	3,558	23.7%	737
51 to 100	3,236	1,363	29.6%	66
101 or more	2,114	1,271	37.5%	21
Total	40,257	13,758	25.5%	15,701

Table 5: Formality and the number of emails from the sender to the recipient, $p < 0.0001$

5.3 Relative power: Rank difference

Another factor that could affect the sender's choice of formality is the relative difference in power or rank between sender and recipient. For example, if a manager sends an email to the CEO of an organization, the email is more likely to be formal than if the recipient has a lower rank than the sender.

To investigate this, we started with the emails in the ISI dataset whose senders are employees appearing in the ISI Enron employee position table and recipients are in the enron.com domain. We grouped the emails by the sender's position and calculated the rate of informality in each group. The results are in Table 6: the first two columns are the title and the rank of the positions in Enron; the third column is the number of employees with that position; the fourth column is the total number of emails sent by these employees; the fifth column is the rate of informality; the last column is the percentage of emails that contain requests according to our request classifier. It is interesting to see that the rates of informality and request vary a lot for different positions; for instance, lawyers are more formal and make more requests than traders.

Position	Rank	# of emp	Emails sent	Inf %	Req %
CEO	6	4	836	19.4%	21.7%
President	5	4	2,680	34.3%	19.3%
VP	4	28	11,425	22.2%	18.1%
Manag Dir	3	6	4,953	14.0%	14.7%
Director	2	22	1,879	29.4%	15.2%
Manager	1	13	6,563	12.4%	25.3%
In-house lawyer	0	3	1,548	7.0%	26.9%
Trader	0	12	1,743	33.1%	13.4%
Employee	0	38	11,770	19.1%	19.1%
Total	-	130	43,397	22.0%	19.2%

Table 6: The set of Enron employees used in the formality vs. rank study

To study the effect of rank difference on formality, we used the first six rows in Table 6 as the relative ranks of the next three rows are not so clearly defined (Diesner et al., 2005). In total, there are 77 employees with rank 1-6, and we call this set of people *RankSet*. We then extracted from the ISI dataset only those emails that have exactly one recipient and both sender and recipient are members of *RankSet*. We grouped this small set, 3999 emails in total, according to the rank difference (which is defined to be the rank of the recipient minus the rank of the sender). The results are in Table 7: the last column is the number of (sender, recipient) pairs with that rank difference. For instance, the -2 row indicates that, among those messages addressed two ranks lower in the organizational hierarchy, 24.7% are informal.

In general, Table 7 shows a lower rate of informality when an email is addressed to a recipient of superior rank. For example, the informality rate of an email addressed to someone 4 or more ranks higher than the sender (15.6%) is less than half that of an email addressed to someone 4 or more ranks lower (31.6%). We do not know what causes the increase of informality from +1 to +2; nevertheless, from +2 to +4 (in emails addressing someone 2-4 ranks higher), there is another decrease in informality rate.

Rank diff	Formal	Inf	Inf %	# of pairs
-4 or less	39	18	31.6%	16
-3	84	32	27.6%	32
-2	226	74	24.7%	56
-1	499	141	22.0%	82
0	989	275	21.8%	190
+1	784	175	18.2%	95
+2	270	121	30.9%	58
+3	125	38	23.3%	46
+4 or more	92	17	15.6%	29
Total	3108	891	22.3%	604

Table 7: Formality and rank difference, $p < 0.0001$. *Rank diff* is equal to recipient rank minus sender rank.

5.4 Weight of imposition: Requests

According to Brown and Levinson's model of politeness, the greater weight of an imposition, the greater the usage of polite speech acts including formality. In this model, a request is one of the most imposing speech acts. Therefore, when a request is made, we would expect a lower rate of informality.

To investigate this, we used the ISI dataset and the results of our request classifier to determine the rate of informality for request and no-request emails. Table 8 shows that there is indeed a lower rate of informality when a request is being made.

	Formal	Informal	Inf %
Request	42,313	9,928	19.0%
No-request	128,958	51,616	28.6%
Total	171,271	61,544	26.4%

Table 8: Formality and request, $p < 0.0001$

# of recipients	Formal	Inf	Inf %
1	70,361	33,115	32.0%
2	5,807	1,914	24.8%
3-5	22,139	4,383	16.5%
6-10	12,903	2,626	16.9%
11 or greater	22,080	5,429	19.7%
Total	133,290	47,467	26.3%

Table 9: Formality and the number of recipients, $p < 0.0001$

5.5 Number of recipients

Another hypothesis we considered is the assumption that a sender is less likely to be informal when there are more recipients on an email since he does not want to broadcast a style which is more personal and could be perceived as unprofessional. To test this hypothesis, we started with the ISI dataset and looked at the subset of emails where an email has at least one recipient.[10] The emails were then grouped based on the number of recipients in the emails.

Table 9 shows the rate of informality with different numbers of recipients. For the most part in these results, a greater number of recipients results in a lower rate of informality. For instance, the rate of informality is nearly cut in half when there are 3 to 5 recipients as opposed to a single recipient. However, at the upper end of this scale, the rate of informality rises again slightly. One possible explanation is that when an email is addressed to a very large number of recipients, the strategies employed (e.g., the model of saving face) might differ from those employed in an email addressed to a small audience.

6 Discussion

In this study, we explored the relation between formality and five factors: (1) personal vs. business, (2) amount of contact, (3) rank difference, (4) request, and (5) number of recipients. The experiments show that the general patterns between the rate of informality and the five factors are consistent with Brown and Levinson's model and our intuition; for instance, an email tends to be more formal if it is about business matter, it is sent to someone with a higher rank, or it contains a request. But the experiments did produce some unexpected results; for instance, the rate of informality increased slightly when the number of recipients is more than 10.

There are several possible reasons for the unexpected results. One is due to the limitation of our dataset. For instance, the social interaction between two people could easily go beyond the 3.5 years covered by the Enron corpus, and people could choose other ways of communication besides email. Therefore, the Enron corpus alone may not be sufficient to capture the social distance between two people in the corpus. Another possible reason is that the errors made by our classifiers could contribute to some of the unexpected results.

The third possible reason, the one that is most interesting to us, is that there are indeed some interesting phenomena which can explain away the unexpectedness of the results. For instance, an email sent to a large number of strangers (e.g., an advertisement sent to a large mailing list) may choose to use an informal and entertaining style in order to catch the recipients' attention. Therefore, a theory that intends to account for people's email behavior may need to distinguish emails sent to a large number of strangers from those sent to a small group of friends. The benefit of a study like ours is that it allows researchers to test a linguistic or social theory on a large data set in a real setting. The study can either provide supporting evidence for a theory or reveal certain discrepancies between the prediction made by the theory and the statistics in the real data, which could lead to revision or refinement of the theory.

While this case study has concentrated on email

[10] Some emails in the ISI dataset do not contain any recipient information. We suspect that the recipient information has been somehow removed before the data was released to the public. With the at-least-one-recipient requirement, the number of non-empty emails in the ISI dataset is reduced from 232,815 to 180,757.

communication, it would be interesting to study formality behavior in other communication media such as Facebook and Twitter. By applying our methodology to other media, it would be possible to determine whether there are other social factors that influence formality on these media. For example, it would be useful to determine whether there is a difference in formality with respect to the number of 'friends' or 'followers' that a person has. Similarly, it would be interesting to examine correlations on the basis of whether a Facebook profile is configured as 'public' or 'private' since the potential viewing audience would be reduced in the case of 'private' profiles. Since Facebook also contains profiles which are associated with both individuals and businesses, it would be interesting to compare these as we did with personal and business emails. Finally, it remains to be seen whether requests could be examined in these media but other social factors (including whether posts related to personal matters, social causes, or event promotion) could be explored to examine formality behavior.

7 Conclusions and Future Work

We believe that NLP techniques can be used to test linguistic or social theories. As a case study, we choose Brown and Levinson's model of politeness (1987), which states that three factors are considered in a decision whether or when to use communication techniques such as formality. We test the theory on the Enron email corpus, and our experimental results are largely consistent with the theory and human intuition.

For future work, we plan to improve the performance of our formality and request classifier by adding additional features such as the ones that look at the layout and zoning of an email (e.g., greetings and signoffs). We also plan to apply our methodology to other genres of data (e.g., blogs, Facebook, Twitter) or to test other theories.

Another direction for future work is to explore what communication techniques such as formality can reveal about the *culture* of a particular social network. For instance, among all the positions listed in the ISI Enron employee position table, lawyers have the lowest rate of informality (7.0%), compared to other positions (e.g., 33.1% for traders). This implies that the workplace behavior of lawyers (at least with respect to emails) is very different from that of traders. It will be interesting to compare the behaviors of people from different occupations or from different social networks. Furthermore, if we could define the norm of behavior within a social group, we could then identify the outliers who might deserve special attention for various reasons.

Acknowledgment We would like to thank Todd Lingren, Chris Rogers and three anonymous reviewers for helpful comments and Katherine Coleman, Carmen Harris and David Horton for providing email annotation. Special thanks are extended to Drew Marrè for his insight in application of this data.

References

Nor Azni Abdullah. 2006. Constructing Business Email Messages: A Model of Writer's Choice. *ESP Malaysia*, 12:53–63.

Steven Bird, Edward Loper, and Ewan Klein. 2009. *Natural Language Processing with Python*. O'Reilly Media Inc.

Penelope Brown and Stephen C. Levinson. 1987. *Politeness: Some Universals in Language Usage*. Cambridge: Cambridge University Press.

Vitor R. Carvalho and William W. Cohen. 2006. Improving "email speech acts" analysis via n-gram selection. In *Proceedings of the Analyzing Conversations in Text and Speech (ACTS) Workshop at HLT-NAACL 2006*, pages 35–41, New York.

Vitor R. Carvalho, Wen Wu, and William W. Cohen. 2007. Discovering leadership roles in email workgroups. In *Proc. of the 4th Conference on Email and Anti-Spam (CEAS 2007)*.

William W. Cohen, Vitor R. Carvalho, and Tom M. Mitchell. 2004. Learning to classify email into "speech acts". In *Proceedings of the EMNLP-2004*, Barcelona, Spain.

A. Culotta, R. Bekkerman, and A. McCallum. 2004. Extracting social networks and contact information from email and the web. In *Proc. of the Conference on Email and Anti-Spam (CEAS 2004)*.

Richard L. Daft and Robert H. Lengel. 1986. Organisational Information Requirements, Media Richness, and Structural Determinants. *Management Science*, 32:554–571.

Jana Diesner, Terill Frantz, and Kathleen Carley. 2005. Communication networks from the enron email corpus "it's always about the people. enron is no different".

Computational & Mathematical Organization Theory, 11(3):201–228.

Sanaz Jabbari, Ben Allison, David Guthrie, and Louise Guthrie. 2006. Towards the Orwellian nightmare: separation of business and personal emails. In *Proceedings of the COLING/ACL 2006 Main Conference Poster Sessions*, pages 407–411.

Parambir S. Keila and David B. Skillcorn. 2005. Detecting unusual and deceptive communication in email. Technical report, Queens University, Ontario, Canada.

Brian Klimt and Yiming Yang. 2004. Enron corpus: A new data set for email classification research. Technical report, Carnegie Mellon University.

Anton Leuski. 2004. Email is a stage: Discovering people roles from email archives. In *Proc. of the 27th Annual International ACM SIGIR Conference on Research and Development in Information Retrieval (SIGIR 2004)*, pages 502–503.

Andrew McCallum, Xuerui Wang, and Andres Corrada-Emmanuel. 2007. Topic and role discovery in social networks with experiments on enron and academic email. *Journal of Artificial Intelligence Research*, 30:249–272.

Andrew McCallum. 2002. Mallet: A machine learning for language toolkit. http://mallet.cs.umass.edu.

Einat Minkov, Richard C. Wang, and WilliamW. Cohen. 2005. Extracting personal names from email: Applying named entity recognition to informal text. In *Proc. of EMNLP-2005*.

Wanda Orlikowski and JoAnne Yates. 1994. Genre repertoire: The structuring of communicative practices in organizations. *Administrative Science Quarterly*, 39(4):541–574.

John R. Searle. 1975. A taxonomy of illocutionary acts. In K. Gunderson, editor, *Language, Mind, and Knowledge*, pages 344–369. Minneapolis.

Jitesh Shetty and Jafar Adibi. 2004. The enron email dataset database schema and brief statistical report. Technical report, Information Sciences Institute at University of South California.

L. Zhou, J.K. Burgoon, J.F. Nunamaker Jr, and D. Twitchel. 2004. Automating linguistics-based cues for detecting deception in text-based asynchronous computer-mediated communication. *Group Decision and Negotiation*, 13:81–106.

Author Index